W9-BXL-025

# MARY HIGGINS CLARK

Mary Higgins Clark. Photograph by Frank Capri. Used with the permission of the photographer.

# MARY HIGGINS CLARK

*A Critical Companion*

Linda C. Pelzer

I.C.C. LIBRARY

CRITICAL COMPANIONS TO POPULAR CONTEMPORARY WRITERS
Kathleen Gregory Klein, Series Editor

Greenwood Press
Westport, Connecticut • London

To my parents,
William and Lois Claycomb

**Library of Congress Cataloging-in-Publication Data**

Pelzer, Linda Claycomb.
    Mary Higgins Clark : a critical companion / Linda C. Pelzer.
        p.    cm.—(Critical companions to popular contemporary
    writers ISSN 1082–4979)
    Includes bibliographical references and index.
    ISBN 0–313–29413–5 (alk. paper)
    1. Clark, Mary Higgins—Criticism and interpretation.
    2. Detective and mystery stories, American—History and criticism.
    I. Title.    II. Series.
    PS3553.L287Z84    1995
    813'.54—dc20            95–4660

British Library Cataloguing in Publication Data is available.

Library of Congress Catalog Card Number: 95–4660
ISBN: 0–313–29413–5
ISSN: 1082–4979

First published in 1995

Greenwood Press, 88 Post Road West, Westport, CT 06881
An imprint of Greenwood Publishing Group, Inc.

Printed in the United States of America

The paper used in this book complies with the
Permanent Paper Standard issued by the National
Information Standards Organization (Z39.48–1984).

10 9 8 7 6 5 4 3 2 1

# Contents

# Contents

# Series Foreword

The authors who appear in the series Critical Companions to Popular Contemporary Writers are all best-selling writers. They do not have only one successful novel, but a string of them. Fans, critics, and specialist readers eagerly anticipate their next book. For some, high cash advances and breakthrough sales figures are automatic; movie deals often follow. Some writers become household names, recognized by almost everyone.

But novels are read one by one. Each reader chooses to start and, more importantly, to finish a book because of what she or he finds there. The real test of a novel is in the satisfaction its readers experience. This series acknowledges the extraordinary involvement of readers and writers in creating a best-seller.

The authors included in this series were chosen by an Advisory Board composed of High School English teachers and High School and Public librarians. They ranked a list of best-selling writers according to their popularity among different groups of readers. Writers in the top-ranked group who had not received book-length, academic literary analysis (or none in at least the past ten years) were chosen for the series. Because of this selection method, Critical Companions to Popular Contemporary Writers meets a need that is not addressed elsewhere.

The volumes in the series are written by scholars with particular expertise in analyzing popular fiction. These specialists add an academic focus on their best-selling writers to the popular success that these writers already enjoy.

The series is designed to appeal to a wide range of readers. The general reading public will find explanations for the appeal of these well-known writers. Fans will find biographical and fictional questions answered. Students will find literary analysis, discussions of fictional genres, carefully organized introductions to new ways of reading the novels, and bibliographies for additional research. Students will also be able to apply what they have learned from this book to their readings of future novels by these best-selling writers.

Each volume begins with a biographical chapter drawing on published information, autobiographies or memoirs, prior interviews, and, in some cases, interviews given especially for this series. A chapter on literary history and genres describes how the author's work fits into a larger literary context. The following chapters analyze the writer's most important, most popular, and most recent novels in detail. Each chapter focuses on a single novel. This approach, suggested by the Advisory Board as the most useful to student research, allows for an in-depth analysis of the writer's fiction. Close and careful readings with numerous examples show readers exactly how the novels work. These chapters are organized around three central elements: plot development (how the story line moves forward), character development (what the reader knows about the important figures), and theme (the significant ideas of the novel). Chapters may also include sections on generic conventions (how the novel is similar to or different from others in its same category of science fiction, fantasy, thriller, etc.), narrative point of view (who tells the story and how), symbols and literary language, and historical or social context. Each chapter ends with an "alternative reading" of the novel. The volume concludes with a primary and secondary bibliography, including reviews.

The Alternative Readings are a unique feature of this series. By demonstrating a particular way of reading each novel, they provide a clear example of how a specific perspective can reveal important aspects of the book. In each alternative reading section, one contemporary literary theory—such as feminist criticism, Marxism, new historicism, deconstruction, or Jungian psychological critique—is defined in brief, easily comprehensible language. That definition is then applied to the novel to highlight specific features that might go unnoticed or be understood differently in a more general reading of the novel. Each volume defines two or three specific theories, making them part of the reader's understanding of how diverse meanings may be constructed from a single novel.

Taken collectively, the volumes in the Critical Companions to Popular Contemporary Writers series provide a wide-ranging investigation of the complexities of current best-selling fiction. By treating these novels seriously as both literary works and publishing successes, the series demonstrates the potential of popular literature in contemporary culture.

Kathleen Gregory Klein
Southern Connecticut State University

# Acknowledgments

Every book is a collaboration, so here I gratefully acknowledge those whose support and assistance made possible my study:

For her gracious cooperation with the project, I owe a special debt of gratitude to Mary Higgins Clark, who agreed to my request for an interview with her. Our discussion of her fiction was both insightful and provocative, reason enough for writing this book. Ms. Lisl Cade, Mrs. Clark's publicist, arranged this interview, and I thank her sincerely for all of her efforts on my behalf.

Colleagues and friends also made valuable contributions to bring this book into existence. Kathleen Gregory Klein, the series editor, suggested the project to me and offered guidance at just the right times. Patty Patterson, Debbie Rickard, and Lorena Stone, my friends and colleagues at Wesley College, listened and responded. Lou Jeffries, librarian at Wesley College, assisted me in my research, and Debbie Seagraves negotiated the maze of my handwritten drafts and transferred them to disk. For coming through in a pinch, Beverly Simpson deserves special mention.

Finally, I thank my husband, John. In countless ways he was there always.

# 1

# "The Queen of Suspense"

Long before she wrote the best-sellers that have earned her the title "Queen of Suspense," Mary Higgins Clark was developing her talent at pajama parties and family gatherings, listening to and learning to spin tales that hypnotized their audience. Storytelling was a chief form of entertainment when she and a host of aunts, great-aunts, and cousins, first and second generation descendants of her Irish grandparents, gathered around the table. The young girl who listened to their tales absorbed them all, and soon she was putting to use what she had learned.

At pajama parties, Clark has confided, "I would tell stories that began: 'Someone—or something—is standing behind that curtain, watching. And his—or its—eyes will fall on one of us. I wonder which one . . . '" (Hoopes 53). From such beginnings was born a storyteller. In fact, Mary Higgins Clark has written eleven best-selling tales of mystery and suspense since the publication in 1975 of her first novel, *Where Are the Children?*

Clark's personal story has its full measure of tragedy and triumph, and it has provided the details of many of her plots and characters. Born in New York City on 24 December 1929, Mary Higgins grew up in the Bronx, where her father, an Irish immigrant, owned the Higgins Bar and Grille. When she was ten years old, she learned the first of a number of hard lessons of life. Returning home from early Mass one morning, she discovered that her beloved father had died in his sleep. Burdened by debt, her mother was left to raise two sons and a daughter. She supported them by working at a series of menial jobs, even though prior to her marriage she had been a chief buyer for the B. Altman department store in Manhattan. Tragedy had struck, but her mother's ability to cope taught Clark resilience and resourcefulness, two characteristics that all her heroines share.

To contribute to the family's income, Mary worked as a babysitter and switchboard operator during high school. Following graduation from Villa Maria Academy, she postponed college to take a secretarial course and worked for several years as an advertising assistant at Remington Rand. One day, however, she abandoned its safe predictability after a friend, a Pan Am stewardess, casually remarked, "God, it was beastly hot in Calcutta." Those seven words changed Clark's life (Freeman 229). Signing on as a Pan Am stewardess, Mary was soon traveling to exotic places. She was also having some frightening adventures. "I was in a revolution in Syria," explains Clark, "and on the last flight into Czechoslovakia before the Iron Curtain went down."

One year after her adventures began, Mary traded in her wings for a wedding band, marrying Warren Clark, a friend of her brother on whom she had had a crush since she was sixteen years old, on 26 December 1949. She and her husband settled in the Stuyvesant Town section of New York to raise the three daughters and two sons who soon filled their house and lives. Simultaneously, Mary began her quest to become a writer. Enrolling in a creative writing course at New York University, she followed the advice of her professor to "write about what you know" (Freeman 231). Drawing on her experience as a stewardess on that last flight to Czechoslovakia, she began her first story, "Stowaway." Six years and forty rejection slips later, Clark sold it to *Extension* magazine for one hundred dollars. When she telephoned her mother to share her success, the ever-practical woman advised her daughter to put her money in the bank. Mary, however, informed her that she intended to spend it and to write other stories, to which her mother responded, "But, Mary, you've used up your idea" (Hoopes 53). Indeed, she had not.

In fact, Mary Higgins Clark had been writing since the age of seven. Her first effort, a poem, had been soundly praised by her mother, "who thought it was beautiful and made me recite it for everyone who came in," Clark recalls. She also wrote plays, which she forced her brothers to perform with her, reserving the starring role for herself (Fakih 36). Throughout the years of her marriage, Clark continued to write stories for national magazines; then, in 1963, the short story market "absolutely went sour." *Collier's* and *Woman's Home Companion* ceased publication, and *Saturday Evening Post* abandoned short stories. "I'm not a *New Yorker* writer," noted Clark, " . . . so that was when I started writing radio shows" (Fakih 36).

The collapse of the short story market, however, was not the only impetus propelling Clark toward a new career. In 1964, Warren Clark suffered his fourth heart attack in five years. It was fatal, and suddenly Mary found herself in the same situation that her own mother had faced years before. She was an impoverished young widow, with five children between the ages of five and thirteen depending upon her. Recognizing that she could not support her family on the income of a freelance writer, Clark took a full-time job writing radio scripts. She continued to work to establish herself as a writer, however, rising early every morning to write for two hours before the children awakened at 7 A.M.

One of Clark's first radio assignments was writing biographical sketches about historical figures for a weekday program called *Portrait of a Patriot*. This "three-year tutorial in history" (Fakih 36), as Clark calls it, led inevitably to a biographical novel as her first attempt at full-length fiction. Published in 1969, *Aspire to the Heavens*, based on the life of George Washington, gave little indication of Clark's future direction as a writer or of the success she would achieve. It was a "commercial disaster and remaindered as it came off the press. But it showed," notes Clark, "that I could write a book and get it published." Mary Higgins Clark was on her way.

Clark's stint as a radio scriptwriter and eventually when she and a partner created Aerial Communications in 1970, as a producer as well, lasted fourteen years and served to some extent as her writing apprenticeship. Producing and writing shows on a variety of topics, from fashion to crime prevention, Clark sharpened her skills. In fact, the demands of radio scriptwriting, especially its fast pacing and believable dialogue, were important to her future in novels. Writing for the radio also helped her to learn "to compress vast amounts of information (or clues)," notes Kimberly Olson Fakih, "into dense, well-placed segments." As Clark herself has noted, "When you have a four-minute program, you learn to write succinctly. . . . Suspense also must move quickly" (Fakih 36).

Despite the fate of her first novel, Clark was determined to succeed. She turned her attention to her own bookshelf as she cast about for a story idea. "I was astonished to realize," she observed, "that ninety percent of the books I'd read in the last couple of years had been mysteries" ("Storyteller" 10). After some additional "soul-digging," Clark began to name her favorite authors, a list that included Mary Roberts Rinehart, Josephine Tey, Agatha Christie, and Charlotte Armstrong. "That was the clue," she realized, "that helped me decide to try a suspense novel" ("Storyteller" 10). Mary Higgins Clark would indeed find success by writing about what she knew best.

Clark's interest in sleuthing and the dark underside of life had begun, she recalls, early in life, with the Bobbsey Twins and the Lindbergh baby kidnapping. She remembers especially the "wonderful solution" (Fakih 36) to the mystery that formed the plot of *The Bobbsey Twins and Baby May*. In that tale, the Bobbseys find an infant abandoned on their doorstep at the same time that an old woman begins to prowl about their home. The twins discover that the old woman, who had just recovered from temporary amnesia, had been the baby's nurse. "A can of soup had hit her on the head and she had forgotten the baby. Once she remembered," says Clark, "she tried to steal the baby back" (Fakih 36). It was, of course, a perfectly reasonable solution to the Bobbseys' puzzle.

Clark recalls as well the haunting power of the Lindbergh baby kidnapping. Long after the event, her parents never let her forget that the kidnappers had deposited their ransom note near the family's summer cottage, which was located near the Throgs Neck Bridge, the tip of the Bronx on Long Island Sound. Each time they passed St. Raymond's Cemetery on their way to their summer retreat, Clark's father reminded his children that at the flower shop across the street from St. Raymond's "the note for that little baby was left" (Fakih 36). From such beginnings was born a writer who, by her own admission, "can't balance a checkbook, but [who] can juggle clues in [her] head" (Hoopes 54).

In 1975, Clark demonstrated her talent for juggling clues in the novel that became her first best-seller, *Where Are the Children?* With its vulnerable heroine and endangered children, the tightly plotted narrative tapped its readers' most basic fears, creating a tense and fast-paced novel of mystery and suspense that climbed quickly to the best-seller lists. Three years later, by the time she had published *A Stranger Is Watching*, Clark had abandoned her radio business to her partner to devote herself full time to writing novels. Today those works have made her one of the most successful popular contemporary writers. Multimillion-dollar book contracts with her publisher, Simon and Schuster, testify to that success. During the summer of 1994, *Remember Me* and *I'll Be Seeing You* simultaneously topped both the hardcover and paperback best-seller lists of the *New York Times* for several weeks, perhaps the best evidence of the degree to which Clark's novels touch her readers.

The success of *Where Are the Children?* provided the widowed mother of five with the financial security to educate not only her children but also herself. In 1974, Clark began to pursue the college degree she had deferred for marriage. In 1979, the forty-nine-year-old author graduated summa cum laude with a Bachelor of Arts degree in philosophy from Fordham University. Nine years later she received an honorary doctorate from her alma mater. She also holds honorary degrees from Villanova University and Rider College. Education has always been important to Mary Higgins Clark, as the invitation to her graduation party testified. On the card Clark had printed, "This invitation is 25 years overdue—help prove it's not too late."

Since the publication of her first best-seller, Clark has produced eleven other equally successful novels of mystery and suspense as well as two collections of short stories. The most recent, *Let Me Call You Sweetheart*, was released in May 1995. Several of her works, including *A Stranger Is Watching* and *Where Are the Children?*, have been made into feature films. Others, such as *The Cradle Will Fall*, *Stillwatch*, and two stories from *The Anastasia Syndrome and Other Stories*, became television films. Clark has also received a number of honors and awards, including the 1992 Irish Woman of the Year Award and France's Grand Prix de Littérature Policière, which she received in 1980. In 1993, she received the Gold Medal of Honor from the American Irish Society, and in 1994, the National Arts Club awarded Clark its first Gold Medal in Education.

Despite a disciplined writing schedule, Clark devotes both time and talent to professional organizations and colleagues. A member of the board of directors and past president of the Mystery Writers of America, she has also served as chairwoman of the International Crime Writers Congress and is an active member of the Society of Magazine Writers and Journalists. Clark is also a founding member of the Adams Round Table, a group of writers that includes Thomas Chastain, Dorothy Salisbury Davis, Justin Scott, and Mickey Friedman. At monthly meetings, members discuss their craft and plot their murders. Occasionally they even collaborate. Already the group has published two collections, *The Case of Caribbean Blues* and *Missing in Manhattan* (1992).

A friend of libraries, Clark is also active in Literacy Volunteers, writing and speaking on behalf of the organization. In fact, she and the other members of the Adams Round Table donated the publisher's advance for *The Case of Caribbean Blues* to the organization. As Clark says, "I don't think it's right for writers to ignore the people who can't read!" (O'Neill 65).

A resident of Saddle River, New Jersey, and New York City, Clark is completing another novel as well as her memoirs, driven by her self-confessed yearning to write ("Storyteller" 10). Recently, she has found some competition rather close to home. Her second daughter, Carol Higgins Clark, has joined her mother on the best-seller lists with her own series of mystery novels featuring serial detective Regan Reilly. Two other children are reported to be plotting as well (Conroy C4). Crime certainly does pay in the Clark family.

Hailed in the 1980s as the modern Agatha Christie, Mary Higgins Clark told an interviewer following the publication of her fifth novel, "Agatha Christie wrote about a hundred books, so I only have 95 to go" (Hoopes 57). Clark's many fans, one suspects, would not object if she equaled that mark.

# 2

# Mary Higgins Clark and the Novel of Suspense

The failure of her biographical novel about George Washington may have been fortunate for Mary Higgins Clark. It was certainly so for her many fans. Although, as she confesses, "I hadn't the faintest idea that I could write suspense" ("Storyteller" 10), she had been educated in the genre by Agatha Christie, Josephine Tey, Mary Roberts Rinehart, and Charlotte Armstrong. Her own reading, in other words, had led her to the genre of which she would soon become a master practitioner.

Suspense novels, notes Joan Aiken, herself a practitioner of the genre, are "very hard to define" (246). Neither spy thriller nor police procedural, they rely on mystery but are not mysteries. In other words, the solution to a puzzle is not the primary focus of the tale. Instead, it focuses on character, a principal element of every novel. Suspense writers place their characters in situations that challenge and even threaten them in order to explore their reactions and reveal their nature and to develop thematic issues.

Clark observes that she writes books that are "neither mystery, nor suspense." Instead, she writes "a *novel* of suspense. I will never win a prize for writing a suspense story," she claims, "because I don't fall into the strict category of suspense." Readers of the genre, however, know that when they open a Mary Higgins Clark novel they will get what they expect: "Something nasty and frightening," according to Aiken, "is bound to happen" (246).

"Suspense," observes John Cawelti, "is essentially the writer's ability to evoke in us a temporary sense of fear and uncertainty about the fate of a character we care about. It is a special kind of uncertainty that is always pointed toward a possible solution" (17). As Mary Higgins Clark explains it, "suspense by its very nature suggests an express train or roller coaster. Once on board, you cannot get off until the ride ends" ("Suspense Writing" 11). To achieve suspense, writers of the genre bring to bear all the elements of the novel and work within long-standing conventions that to some extent define the genre. Among the most important elements are plot, character, and setting.

## PLOT

At the heart of virtually every novel of suspense is a situation that threatens the protagonist, or central character. The situation need not be a mystery, a hidden secret or confusing puzzle that must be exposed or solved. It frequently is, however, because mystery "can intensify and complicate a story of triumph over obstacles or of the successful development of love by increasing suspense and uncertainty and adding further interest to the final resolution" (Cawelti 43). Typically, the plot of a novel by Mary Higgins Clark is a combination of mystery and suspense, with suspense predominating. In her first novel, *Where Are the Children?*, a mother who had been accused of murdering her children is the chief suspect seven years later when her children from a later marriage also go missing. Embedded in the frantic search for the children is the solution to the mystery of the first murders, but the immediate source of the novel's appeal is the suspense generated by the search. Readers know almost from the beginning the identity of the kidnapper. They know as well his malevolent reasons for abducting the children because they have been inside his twisted mind. Yet the novel's basic plot, the frantic search for endangered children, drives readers relentlessly to the horrifying confrontation between the forces of good and evil and the satisfying resolution of the terror. Despite their early understanding of the novel's mystery, readers need to know the outcome of the heroine's ordeal, so they keep turning the pages.

One other typical element of the suspense novel is romance. Because her narratives of mystery, secrets, and suspense inevitably include a love interest, some define the genre in which she writes as romantic suspense. Clark herself does not. Granted, "there's always," as she notes, "an important, strong man" (O'Neill 64) in her fiction, and that man typically arrives at the climax of the novel to assist the heroine in her struggle with the forces of evil. But the love interest, although a requisite element of romantic suspense, is always a subplot in a Clark novel, subordinated to the primary tale of an endangered heroine who must overcome obstacles primarily by herself. As Clark observes, "The love interest is incidental to the plot. The plot doesn't turn on it."

## CHARACTER

This emphasis on the heroine's struggle indicates the importance of character to the suspense novel. Unlike the classical mystery or detective novel, which is, according to Kathleen Gregory Klein, "primarily a puzzle or intellectual game where minimal attention is paid to the sufferings of the victim or even the probable fate of the criminal" (4), the suspense novel depends upon fully realized characters for its effect. "The conflict [in suspense] is on an individual, adversarial level," according to Aiken. "The hero/heroine is pitted not against organized crime or international terrorism, but against a personal enemy, a personal problem." Thus, "if either hero or hero's enemy is not a flesh-and-blood, fully rounded, recognizable entity, the tension slackens, the credulity drops" (Aiken 247).

In the hands of Mary Higgins Clark, both heroine and villain are clearly defined, and she leaves no doubt about which role her characters play. Clark confesses that she is "not comfortable with the non-hero or non-heroine who is basically so bad-tempered or self-serving that in real life I would avoid him or her like the plague." Nor does she "get emotional satisfaction out of a book in which the villain is so desperately attractive that I find myself rooting for him to beat the system." Clark prefers instead "to write about *very* nice people who are confronted by the forces of evil and who through their own courage and intelligence work their way through to deliverance" ("Suspense Writing" 11).

Clark's heroine is typical of the genre: She is resilient, resourceful, and absolutely determined to overcome the menace and even the physical dangers that threaten her. Like her historical antecedents, Charlotte Brontë's Jane Eyre or the narrator of Daphne du Maurier's *Rebecca*, she has about her an air of vulnerability that hints at the personal pain or unhappiness in her past. That impression, however, belies the strength of character upon which she draws to meet the challenges of life. Although she suffers from post-traumatic stress syndrome, Menley Nichols, the heroine of Clark's 1994 novel *Remember Me*, manages to escape murder by feigning her drowning, and Menley is merely the most recent in a whole series of Clark heroines who overcome similar dangers. Clark describes her heroines as "strong, but not tough."

While Clark's heroine is physically attractive, her real attraction arises from her strength of being. Neither introverted nor self-centered, she possesses an innate intelligence and a deepening self-awareness. She is also kind and considerate to everyone she meets, and her compassion for others draws sympathetic responses from all. Attracted to men who share her own qualities, including a sense of humor, she values in them, according to Barbara Norville, "the very facets that she likes in herself, or that the reader sees in her, which contribute toward making a whole person" (39). Above all, however, she possesses "a firm sense of her own value and clear values by which she judges the world" (40). Those qualities evoke the reader's sympathy and identification.

Clark's heroine is, of course, a romantic. She believes in goodness and rightness, and her own optimistic faith that they will prevail leads her to pursue the truth. But she is also a realist capable of evaluating other people and her situation and taking appropriate action. Like other heroines of the genre, "she does call upon some of the men in her life to help her, but the initiative lies with her and the men are part of a plan, not a first resort" (Norville 40). Ultimately, the heroine's triumph over evil supports her optimistic faith and demonstrates that she is not naive. Her belief in the good and the right, in other words, is tempered by a mature recognition and understanding of their opposites.

If Clark's heroine embodies goodness, then her villain certainly makes real moral corruption and wickedness, and Clark takes great care to provide him with psychological motivation, however twisted. Her villains are kidnappers, serial killers, child molesters, and megalomaniacs all who prey on the weak and vulnerable. Clark notes that her villains "are, and probably will continue to be, as evil, as frightening, as quietly vicious as I can dream them up" ("Suspense Writing" 11).

## SETTING

"The better formulaic artists," according to Cawelti, "devise means of protracting and complicating suspense" (17). These twists and turns of plot and character withhold from readers the resolution of uncertainty and menace that is characteristic of the suspense novel. Clark also relies on another narrative element, setting, as an "essential [contributor] to a successful suspense novel" ("Suspense Writing" 10).

Clark is adept at using time and place to heighten the tension of her fiction, frequently investing buildings with appropriate atmosphere and symbolic resonance. For example, both Remember House, the site of *Remember Me*, and the Minnesota farmstead of *A Cry in the Night* are inhabited by ghosts, which haunt their rooms and corridors just as they do their characters' minds. Similarly, Grand Central Station, a bustling hub of activity, serves as a prison for kidnapping victims and thereby provides an ironic edge to *A Stranger Is Watching*. Clark also uses the stark, clinical corridors of modern hospitals to emphasize the terror of science gone wrong in *The Cradle Will Fall* and *I'll Be Seeing You*. Whether her story takes place at a luxurious spa, on a weather-beaten island, or even in midtown Manhattan, Clark finds just the right details to enhance the atmosphere of foreboding and terror.

Perhaps more important than place, however, is time, for as Clark notes, "the containment of time makes for more excitement" (O'Neill 64). Clark confines all of her tales to a limited time frame—a weekend, a week, seldom longer than a month—and from the beginning of the novel, readers know that a dangerous deadline is rapidly approaching for the heroine. The serial killer in *Loves Music, Loves to Dance*, for example, plans to murder his final victim on the fifteenth anniversary of the murder of his first victim. That deadline, of which the indomitable heroine is unaware, looms menacingly in the future of Darcy Scott, and as each day advances toward it, Clark raises the novel's level of tension to propel readers toward the climax. Similarly, in *A Stranger Is Watching*, readers share the anxiety of the central characters, who wait, seemingly powerless, for a bomb to explode and the execution of an innocent man. Clark believes that "the suspense is considerably greater" in a book in which "people are kidnapped and the villain plans to execute them at a specific time" than in a book in which "the reader is only generally concerned about the victims' welfare" ("Suspense Writing" 10). Consequently, she uses the clock to great effect.

## CLARK'S BODY OF WORK

With the publication of her first successful novel, *Where Are the Children?*, Clark demonstrated her skill in using the conventions of the mystery-suspense genre, and she continues to do so today. "Right from the beginning," notes Thomas Whissen, "Clark established herself as anything but a mere spinner of suspense novels about distraught heroines menaced by villains and rescued by Mr. Right." Instead, the resourceful heroine of that first novel, "an ordinary woman driven by terrifying circumstances to do extraordinary things" (Whissen 67), became the standard for all of the others. Clark duplicated and then replicated her in *A Stranger Is Watching* (1978) and *The Cradle Will Fall* (1980), her second and third novels, and in every novel since.

If her heroine has remained essentially the same from novel to novel, Clark's plots certainly have not. Beginning with *The Cradle Will Fall*, a medical thriller in the tradition of Robin Cook, Clark "embarked," according to Whissen, "on a series of experimental novels in which she tried her hand at types of mystery fiction usually associated with other popular writers" (67). Her fourth novel, *A Cry in the Night* (1982), is a modern tale of gothic suspense. Complete with the traditional elements of the genre—a brooding hero, a ghostly presence, and a mysterious mansion in which the seemingly unexplainable occurs—it is every bit as compelling as Daphne du Maurier's *Rebecca*, one of its forebears. *Stillwatch* (1984), a political thriller, or tale of intrigue set amid the corridors of governmental power, explores territory familiar to readers of Margaret Truman. The haunting tale interweaves the lives of a senator about to be appointed the first woman vice-president and the television journalist who is producing a news feature about her. In *Weep No More, My Lady* (1987), written in the tradition of Thomas Tryon, Clark published a "celebrity" mystery. In it, she examines the lives of movie stars and other rich and famous people to expose their dark underside. Each of these novels stands on its own merits as an example of its kind, and most compete favorably with their counterparts by other practitioners of the genres, such as Truman, Cook, and Tryon. With her next four novels, however, Clark found the subjects and settings that were truly her own.

Set almost exclusively in New York City, these novels feature "a savvier breed of heroine" (Whissen 67) and a contemporary edge that mirror the increasingly complex and cosmopolitan society of late twentieth-century urban America. The protagonists of these novels tend to be professional women of wit and intelligence who move in sophisticated circles. *While My Pretty One Sleeps* (1989), the first of these four novels, explores the competitive world of high fashion. *Loves Music, Loves to Dance* (1991) features two Manhattan career women struggling to establish themselves—and to survive—in an environment hostile to the uninitiated.

In their subject matter, these novels demonstrate as well Clark's ability to tackle contemporary issues with candor and sensitivity. *Loves Music, Loves to Dance*, a hard-hitting novel reminiscent of Judith Rossner's *Looking for Mr. Goodbar*, focuses on the risks involved in personal ad dating. *All Around the Town* (1992) combines the issue of child abuse with the enigma of multiple personality disorder. The final novel in this group, *I'll Be Seeing You* (1993), returns to a topic Clark had previously explored in *The Cradle Will Fall*, reproduction technology. The complex and controversial subjects of these novels provide Clark with the opportunity to combine a good read with critical insight into contemporary fears and disillusionment, anxiety and alienation.

*Remember Me* (1994) marks a departure from the sophisticated urban settings and contemporary social issues that have defined Clark's most recent work. In this novel, Clark ventures again into the realm of the gothic and supernatural, territory she previously explored in *A Cry in the Night* and the novella *The Anastasia Syndrome* (1989). She creates a psychological thriller that links treatment of post-traumatic stress syndrome and Alzheimer's disease to a ghost story. More successful than either of the previous works, *Remember Me* gives evidence of Clark's assured handling of her material and her mature treatment of the themes and concerns that have come to dominate her work.

Several of those themes surface again in *Let Me Call You Sweetheart* (1995), Clark's twelfth best-selling novel of mystery and suspense. In this work, she returns as well to the professional, urban world with which she is most familiar, this time to write a tale of obsessive love and betrayal. Mystery rather than suspense dominates the novel, and yet the shift in emphasis has not diminished Clark's ability, as Marilyn Stasio notes in her review of the work, to use language "so light on its feet that it races the story straight for the cliffs on which every chapter ending hangs" (24).

Although she has founded her reputation on her novels, Clark has also ventured into the realm of the short story, publishing two collections during her career. *The Anastasia Syndrome and Other Stories* (1989), in addition to its title novella, a tale of psychological possession, contains three stories that epitomize Clark's style. They are, as Bill Kent notes, "trim, tidy, edge-of-the-seat crowd pleasers in which the heroines are all innocent, decent, beautiful women menaced by familiar types: a scheming pervert, a frustrated actor, an untrustworthy husband" (82). The collection's best entry, "Terror Stalks the Class Reunion," a tale of psychopathic obsession that nearly turns disastrous, is "pure, gut-wrenching suspense" (Kent 82), just what Clark's readers expect.

In *The Lottery Winner: Alvirah and Willy Stories* (1994), Clark resurrects

Alvirah Meehan, the former cleaning woman who won 40 million dollars in the lottery and then, indulging a whim, headed for Cypress Point Spa, the setting of *Weep No More, My Lady*. A good-hearted but rather unlikely client among the spa's rich and famous, Alvirah turns amateur sleuth to help solve several murders, barely escaping the killer herself. Alvirah is clearly a favorite character, for Clark had poisoned her off in a first draft of a novella, but allowed her to recover at the urging of her daughter Carol (Conroy C4). In *The Lottery Winner*, the ever-resourceful Alvirah and her dependable husband Willy find themselves escaping danger and solving crimes in stories characterized by gentle humor and subtle wit, qualities that Clark is rarely able to infuse into her novels given their horrifying situations and serious subject matter.

## MAJOR THEMES

The development of Clark's body of work demonstrates not only the skill with which she handles narrative elements but also the psychological insight she brings to her major themes and concerns. Just as her technical ability has sharpened during her career, so, too, has her treatment of her subjects deepened and matured. Her early novels, for instance, were concerned almost exclusively with the interconnections between the past and the present. Again and again Clark's heroines suffer because they refuse to face the past that haunts them. The past nearly repeats itself because Nancy Harmon, the heroine of *Where Are the Children?*, has repressed its painful truths. Similarly, Pat Traymore, the heroine of *Stillwatch*, nearly falls victim to a killer because she, too, cannot remember the knowledge that would save her. The continuing presence of the past is a constant theme in Clark's fiction, serving as a foundation on which to erect related themes.

One of these themes is the struggle toward selfhood, which figures prominently in the majority of Clark's novels. Clark's heroines, most of whom are in their mid- to late twenties, are self-aware but not entirely self-defined. They may have a strong sense of self, or at least give the appearance of utter self-assurance, but they are still capable of growth. In fact, they need to grow. Even a competent lawyer like Katie DeMaio in *The Cradle Will Fall* or a professional television journalist like Meghan Collins in *I'll Be Seeing You* achieves a new maturity and a deepened sense of self by confronting the ghosts of the past. When they triumph over the doubts, fears, and pain that reside in the dark recesses of their minds and souls, Clark's heroines reveal their capacity for growth.

Clark links her heroines' struggle toward self-awareness and self-definition to a theme that gains increasing importance in her novels, the complexity of the parent-child relationship. While this theme lies beneath the surface of her first novel, *Where Are the Children?*, in Nancy Harmon's relationship with her first husband, Carl, Clark leaves it largely unexplored. With each novel, however, the theme assumes more prominence, and by the time Clark writes the four novels that reflect her competence and maturity as a master of suspense, the parent-child theme dominates all others. In this group of novels, beginning with *While My Pretty One Sleeps* and ending with *I'll Be Seeing You*, Clark exposes with increasing candor and psychological insight the legacies of the parent-child relationship in the lives of all adults. This theme is clearly important to Clark, who admits that she wrote *While My Pretty One Sleeps* with the intention of portraying a "strong father-daughter relationship" (*Loves Music* interview n. p.). Such a positive view of the family relationship lies behind Clark's exploration of the theme, even if the relationships themselves do not always support this perspective. It is this basic opposition, in fact, between intent and execution that makes Clark's treatment of the theme so evocative and provocative.

At the end of a Mary Higgins Clark novel of suspense, readers can take satisfaction in the restoration of order and rationality to an otherwise chaotic world where evil invades even the lives of the most innocent and good. That reassurance of order may be just what Clark's readers seek from her tales. Clark herself acknowledges this appeal:

> People can walk into the shoes of my characters. We all hang by a thread and there are many things we cannot choose about our lives. It's how we react to the inevitable that counts. My characters are strong. When calamity strikes they react well. They keep going, they carry on. At the end of a suspense novel or a mystery the problem is solved, the culprit is punished, satisfaction has been taken for the victim's life. And I think there is a sense of harmony that we too often don't find in life. (Hoopes 56)

In the end, Clark's positive world view and strong human values give substance to her suspense thrillers and offer hope to us all.

# 3

# *Where Are the Children?*
## (1975)

Mary Higgins Clark's first novel of suspense, *Where Are the Children?*, was also her first best-seller, and the reasons for its success are clear. Drawing her plot from the headlines and evoking a contemporary social issue, Clark tapped into the deepest fears of her readers. She forced them to confront the underside of their ordinary lives and to acknowledge the evil lurking in the shadows of their quiet existence. A vulnerable heroine and children in peril combined with other elements of the novel to propel readers to its terrifying climax. This powerful mixture, with slight variations, would drive her subsequent novels to the best-seller lists as well.

*Where Are the Children?* is the story of Nancy Harmon, a woman whose past holds a terrible secret. Seven years before the events in the novel, Nancy was convicted of murdering her two little children but released on a legal technicality. Abandoning the pain of that old life, she fled the notoriety generated by the hostile front-page newspaper stories about the crime. She changed her name, dyed her red hair sable brown, and left San Francisco for the peace and privacy of Cape Cod. Now Nancy is married to Ray Eldredge, has two more beloved children, Michael and Missy, and has begun to trust her new happiness and to look tentatively toward the future. On the morning of her thirty-second birthday, however, the nightmare of the past begins again. Nancy looks in the backyard for her little boy and girl and finds only one red mitten. The frantic search for Michael and Missy that drives the novel's plot will ultimately expose the truth about both the darkest of crimes and the mysteries of self.

## NARRATIVE STRATEGIES TO CREATE MYSTERY AND SUSPENSE: PLOT AND SETTING

### Plot

One of the requirements of a novel of suspense is a plot that places its protagonist, or central character, in threatening situations, and *Where Are the Children?* certainly has that. The novel was inspired by the 1965 Alice Crimmins case, in which a Queens, New York, mother reported the disappearance of her two small children. When they were found murdered, an extensive investigation led to Crimmins' arrest. Following two lengthy trials, she was convicted of killing her children. The motive for the crime was apparently to prevent her estranged husband from gaining custody of them.

The plot of Clark's novel is quite different from the case that inspired it, for readers know the identity of the criminal almost from the beginning. So skillful is Clark at creating suspense, however, that readers race to the novel's conclusion. "The theme of a missing child," Clark explained in an interview, "struck a personal chord in me" (*Loves Music* interview n.p.). In her essay "Suspense Writing," Clark explained her fascination in more detail: "I had five children, and the thought of losing any of them gave me nightmares. The thought of not only losing them but being accused of *murdering* them was beyond comprehension. A voice in my subconscious whispered, 'And then suppose it happened again?' *Where Are the Children?* was in gestation" (10).

Clark creates suspense in *Where Are the Children?* not only through its subject matter, but also by skillfully interweaving simultaneous episodes. The Prologue takes readers into the twisted mind of an unknown stalker, immediately establishing the novel's tone of menace. Four chapters later, after he has exposed Nancy Eldredge's secret in the local newspaper, the villain is once again the focus, this time as he congratulates himself about the perfection of his plan. In the meantime, Clark begins to introduce her cast of characters: Nancy; her husband, Ray, a realtor; his secretary, Dorothy Prentiss; and Jonathan Knowles, the retired lawyer who is writing a book on famous murder trials, including the Harmon case. All will play their part in the drama about to unfold, but none of them senses the immediate danger readers know exists.

This episodic plot structure, or series of connected incidents, is especially effective in the chapters detailing Nancy's drug-induced exploration of the secrets buried deep within her mind. So crucial are Nancy's memories to the solution of all the novel's mysteries that readers want to rush through her painful confession. Clark makes such efforts impossible, prolonging the suspense by extending this episode over two chapters. She also interrupts Nancy's tale with a long chapter during which Dorothy shows The Lookout, the villain's base of operations, to a prospective buyer and the children come tantalizingly close to being discovered. Clark also withholds Nancy's final, crucial memory until Chapter 28, three chapters from the novel's horrifying climax. In other words, Clark plays her hand slowly, one card at a time. She understands the thrill of anticipation.

## Setting

Clark also makes effective use of setting, and especially the unities of time and place, to heighten the suspense of *Where Are the Children?* The lonely isolation of Cape Cod in mid-November, for example, in addition to lending credibility to the events, emphasizes the plaintiveness of Nancy's plight. In spite of the loving support of friends and husband, Clark's heroine must face her inner demons if she is to triumph over the evil that has seized control of her life. Hers is a solitary battle, made even more difficult by the forces of nature, which seem to conspire against her.

Throughout the novel, a violent storm has been threatening, and as the events rush to their climax, the vicious winds vent their full force, and treacherous sleet blankets the landscape. This upheaval in nature signifies the violation in human relationships that drives the novel's plot. It also corresponds to the turmoil of the heroine's psychological landscape. Nancy must fight not only the physical forces that threaten her existence but also her inner demons.

Finally, the action of *Where Are the Children?* takes place on one day, a constriction of time that functions both technically and thematically. In the first instance, it intensifies the pace of the plot: so much happens in so little time. In the second instance, the events occur on Nancy's birthday. While the day should be an occasion for celebration, it is instead for Nancy a day of mourning, for it is also the seventh anniversary of the death of her children, Peter and Lisa. Life and death are thus inextricably connected on this day of beginnings, and Nancy's actions on this day will determine whether she dies another death or is reborn.


## CHARACTER DEVELOPMENT

Clark's skillful handling of the elements of plot and setting creates much of the novel's suspense. Her ability to develop believable characters about whom readers care lends emotional weight to her structure and supports her thematic concerns. Clark writes, as she says, about "nice people whose lives are invaded by evil. They are people with whom we can identify" (*Loves Music* interview n.p.). Such identification helps to explain the appeal of Nancy Eldredge, a loving wife and caring mother, utterly undeserving of her horrifying fate. She lives, and thereby confirms, the nightmare Clark's readers dread for themselves.

Nancy Eldredge is the perfect victim, for she is living a lie and fears exposure. She has changed her physical appearance, cutting and dyeing her hair and abandoning the childish dresses her first husband, Carl, had liked her to wear for tailored styles that express her own taste. The real Nancy, however, lies buried deep within her heart and mind. The horrors of the past have left her psychologically and emotionally scarred, and she is aware that "a part of her was still frozen" (*Where Are the Children?* 10). For years she has hidden her true self just as she has hidden the watercolors she paints, but on her thirty-second birthday Nancy seems willing to heed the advice of her sympathetic husband Ray and put the past behind her: "*Seven years*, Nancy thought. Life was a series of seven-year cycles. Carl used to say that your whole body changed in that time. Every cell renewed itself. It was time for her to really look ahead . . . to forget" (10). Nancy's decision, however, lacks the force of self necessary to realize it, for as Clark reveals her heroine's past, it is clear that Nancy's new identity is as tenuous as her old one.

Although the key to the present lies in the past, the disappearance of Michael and Missy and the pain of the long-repressed memories of her previous existence cause Nancy to slip into hysterical amnesia. Only under the effect of sodium amytal and the gentle questioning of Dr. Lendon Miles, a psychiatrist who feels that he failed her once before, can Nancy divulge the truth. What she reveals is truly shocking. Many years before, Nancy Harmon had also been a victim.

The eighteen-year-old Nancy who had left her Ohio home to attend college in San Francisco had been eager for life. Although she worried about her widowed mother, Priscilla Kiernan, to whom she was deeply attached, both women had accepted the challenges of their new beginnings. Nancy's mother had fallen in love with her employer, Lendon Miles. Nancy had made friends, was dating frequently, and was doing well with her studies—except for biology. When Carl Harmon, her professor, offered to tutor her, Nancy had no way of knowing the extent to which he would soon be guiding her life.

Under the effect of sodium amytal, Nancy reluctantly exposes the secrets of her relationship with Harmon. He insisted, for instance, that she stop dating to improve her grades and that she take the vitamins he prescribed for her even though they made her tired and disoriented. Soon he was selecting childish dresses for her to wear. After the too convenient accidental death of her mother, Harmon almost seemed to seize control of her will. Within months after her arrival in San Francisco, Nancy found herself married to Harmon, a man intent upon taking care of her.

But Carl's "goodness" and caring were not at all what they appeared to be. They were, in fact, the self-absorbed cruelties of the pedophile, the child molester. This is the stark reality, the cruel truth that Nancy has so deeply repressed. The innocent young woman who trusted her biology professor had become a sexually abused wife. Eventually, fearing that her toddler, Lisa, had become her husband's next victim, Nancy put into motion the events that would lead to the murder of her children, the "suicide" of a respected academic, and the charges against her.

Knowledge of the past gives Nancy the power not only to rewrite the ending to her story but also to reclaim her self. Her understanding has come too late to save Peter and Lisa, the children of her marriage to Carl. It comes just soon enough, however, to rescue Michael and Missy from the clutches of the man determined first to possess her and then, failing that, to destroy her. Realizing the identity of their abductor, and aided by her friend Dorothy's discovery of a second red mitten, Nancy confronts Carl Harmon and in hand-to-hand combat wrests her children and her self from insidious evil.

Nancy Eldredge has earned her birthday by the novel's end. Her sleeping life is over. No longer is she in need of Carl. Rather, she is a woman capable of facing adult realities. She now acknowledges her own sexuality and mutual desire for the husband who shares her life (250). She is now tough and resilient enough to survive whatever life may bring. On her thirty-second birthday, Nancy Eldredge asserts her self and lives; to signify this act, Clark promises her readers that her heroine will once again be the redhead she was born as.

Although Clark focuses her characterization on the emotional and psychological landscape of the victim, her portrayal of the victimizer is equally compelling. In Carl Harmon, Clark gives her readers a chilling depiction of the sociopath. He is so adept at hiding his antisocial behavior that everyone sees only a respected professor, a devoted husband, and a grieving father driven to suicide rather than a deeply disturbed pedophile capable of murder. Like Nancy, Carl, too, is living a lie, but whereas exposure saves the victim, it destroys the victimizer.

Clark's explanation for Harmon's psychosexual abnormality is rather simplistic—his hatred of women, who could be "sly" (3). Her depiction of his criminal behavior, however, is chillingly real and therefore disturbing. Harmon takes pleasure in giving pain. He enjoys his power to expose Nancy's past and thereby destroy her. He revels in the "audacity" of his plan (35). From the safety of The Lookout, the seventeenth-century captain's house that he sarcastically considers "a pretentious monument to man's need to be forever on guard" (2), Harmon has nothing but contempt for the ordinary people of the world, seeing them as capable only of victimization.

Central to the depiction of both Nancy and Carl is the metaphor of disguise. Clark uses this figure of speech to draw a comparison between physical appearance and inner being. Both characters have altered their physical appearance to avoid detection, yet neither is able to disguise his or her inner being. Nancy may have dyed her strawberry curls deep sable, but when Carl spies upon her with his high-powered telescope, he cannot deny her "intriguing young quality, soft and fresh and silky" (5). Nancy cannot mask an innocence and vulnerability that signify her essential goodness. And Ray also knows her innate "distaste for ugliness" (158). Nancy Harmon Eldredge, in whatever guise, is simply incapable of murder.

Similarly, Carl disguises his identity, but not his essence. During the six years that he has been stalking Nancy, waiting for his opportunity to destroy her again, Carl has deliberately put on layers of fat. Now "his thick, trunklike legs [are] tight in shiny black trousers" (4), and a heavy stench of perspiration, the sour smell of fear, clings to him. He is gross and repulsive even to himself and eagerly anticipates the time when he can shed his mass of flesh and resume a normal life (4). Carl, however, is incapable of such a life, and his mass of flesh is anything but a disguise. This is a man whose appetites consume others, who grows fat on their suffering. He is what he appears to be.


## THEMATIC ISSUES

All of the supporting characters in *Where Are the Children?* are believable, but none is as fully developed as Nancy and Carl, and this emphasis suggests the novel's thematic concerns. Certainly Clark's novel explores the nature of evil, its sinister power, its subtle treachery, its reality. Carl Harmon embodies every dark intent, every wicked impulse of which humans are capable. The adult who preys on children is especially despised within our culture. Thus, Carl's crime, pedophilia, and his pleasure in it prevent readers from developing any sympathy for this villain. Unadulterated evil, Clark seems to say, may exist, but it need not be tolerated. In fact, true goodness can defeat it, as Nancy Eldredge does.

To combat evil, however, we must first acknowledge its reality, and that Nancy Eldredge had failed to do. She had refused to face the truth of her fears—that Carl had murdered her mother, that he had sexually abused her and her daughter, that his goodness was actually cruelty. Instead, Nancy allowed her husband to take care of her, to keep her in a state of perpetual but artificial childhood that prevented her from attaining true adulthood. And when reality became too unbearable, she had simply "dropped a protective curtain over painful memories" (10) to survive. Only when she is willing to lift the veil from the past does Nancy cease to be haunted by it. Only then is she released from the doom of repeating it. Knowledge gives her the power to prevail.

Such knowledge, Clark makes clear, is not limited simply to knowledge of other lives and other realities. It includes as well—and perhaps more importantly—knowledge of self, and here again, Nancy Eldredge is lacking. At thirty-two she is still too much the child. Observing his wife after pulling her from the icy pond in which she has been frantically searching for her children, Ray thinks of Nancy as "curiously small and inert inside [her robe]—not unlike a child herself" (10). So limited is her self-awareness that she has almost begun to believe that she did indeed murder her children. "How could I have killed them?" (132), Nancy anguishes under the effect of sodium amytal, a seeming confession that indicates that she, too, is one of the lost children of the novel's title.

Nancy's triumph over Carl Harmon is, then, the result of a conscious decision to know, to become an adult capable of saving both herself and her children. As she says when she agrees to the sodium amytal treatment, "I have to know. . . . If there is some awful part of me that could hurt my children . . . we have to know that too" (122). In Nancy's triumph, Clark clearly demonstrates that the key to the mysteries of life and death, good and evil, lies within the dark recesses of the self.

## A FEMINIST READING OF *WHERE ARE THE CHILDREN?*

Feminist critics reading *Where Are the Children?* might also emphasize the psychology of the heroine, viewing her psychological landscape from the perspective of gender differences and gender expectations. They would focus, in other words, on issues of control, especially as they limit a woman's sense of power and authority over her own existence. To understand such a perspective we need first to consider the word "feminism," a term everyone recognizes but one that few can define clearly and with uniform agreement. Feminist criticism does not include all literary criticism written by women, since not all women are feminists, nor does it include all criticism written by feminists, since feminists may view a literary work from any theoretical perspective. The characteristic common to feminist criticism is its concern for the impact of gender on reading and writing. To determine that impact, it examines not only the concerns of literature, but also sociological, political, and economic ideas. "The feminist critique," as Elaine Showalter observes, "is essentially political and polemical" ("Poetics" 129), and thus it suggests alternatives to tradition.

Histories of feminist criticism usually divide it into three broad phases. The first involves analysis of patriarchal culture, a term for the institutions, attitudes, and beliefs of a society dominated by men. In the field of literary criticism, this analysis or critique has taken the form of exposing what Showalter calls "the misogyny of literary practice," the explicit and implicit prejudices in male writing about women. Such practices include, according to Showalter, "the stereotyped images of women in literature as angels or monsters, the literary abuse or textual harassment of women in classics and popular male literature, and the exclusion of women from literary history" ("Revolution" 5). This feminist critique examines as well the woman as reader of works by men and by other women, exploring the way in which "the hypothesis of a female reader changes our apprehension of" the literary text ("Poetics"

128). This feminist critique has led to enlightening new interpretations of classics previously evaluated only by male critics with traditional attitudes. Some critics, however, caution against the potential dangers of such readings, arguing that the social and historical contexts of a literary work are essential to understanding the author's choices. For example, it is unfair for a contemporary feminist critic to berate Chaucer for failing to make the Wife of Bath a lawyer, because women professionals did not exist in his time. But when applied to contemporary works of literature, this feminist critique yields some surprising debate as both male and female critics comment on the same work—frequently with remarkably different conclusions.

The second phase of feminist literary criticism might be characterized by what Showalter has termed "gynocritics," or a concern with women as writers giving expression to the female experience through their work ("Poetics" 128–129). Discovering that women writers had a literature of their own, gynocritics set out to map the territory of the female imagination. They sought to define the distinctive mode of discourse, or means of communication, that distinguished women's texts from men's. This focus of gynocritics led to the recovery of many forgotten works by women. It led as well to a new understanding of the struggles women writers faced to express their own visions and experiences in a patriarchal society that discounted them.

Both of these aspects of feminism constitute what in recent years has been termed "gender studies." Both also share the idea that gender difference determines much about a person's life experience and thus about one's means of communicating, reading, or writing. A third phase of feminism focuses on the similarities between men and women and argues that emphasizing differences is a tactic used by men to exclude and oppress women. These critics stress instead the humanity of all people, regardless of gender. They believe that the only way to achieve equality is to deny that there are fundamental differences between men and women. In fact, these egalitarian feminists fear that the emphasis on difference weakens feminism because it produces a kind of reverse discrimination and stereotyping—everything male is negative, and everything female is positive. The egalitarian feminists believe that the narrow focus of gender studies critics leads to their isolation in the critical debate and thus their effectual silencing. Consequently, they promote the shared experience of all people as the foundation of real equality and understanding.

Whatever their critical stance, feminists do seem to share one important idea about literary criticism: the impossibility of achieving objectivity. For years, critics believed that the author's personal history, the social expectations of his or her time, and the historical events that transpired during the author's life had no bearing on understanding literary works. Instead, literature was a world of its own, complete in itself, and thus could be evaluated without reference to personal, social, and historical context. Feminist critics believe that such objectivity is impossible. Instead, they promote subjectivity, responses based on experience and belief. They recognize that every reader brings both to the literary work and thus understands literature from a personal perspective.

As a book written by a woman about a woman protagonist, *Where Are the Children?* yields some provocative insights if viewed from the perspective of a gynocritic. The novel clearly suggests that Nancy is a victim of patriarchy, of a society that teaches women to defer to men and that encourages them to depend upon men for their well-being. Although Nancy's father is dead, for instance, and therefore unable to participate in her life, his absence makes her vulnerable to Carl Harmon. Not only is he unable to protect his daughter from this predator, but his absence also leads her to search for a replacement for him. As the first man in his daughter's life, the father exerts tremendous power. As Lynda E. Boose notes, he is the "chief authorizing figure and primary model for the daughter's later male relationships" (38). He is also the ideal symbol of patriarchy.

Nancy's memories of life with her father, revealed when she is under the influence of sodium amytal, are loving and carefree, and they indicate the deep psychological need that the daughter develops for the father. Remembering a generous man who was "such fun" (*Children?* 156), Nancy speaks with an uncharacteristic "lilt" in her voice. She is "animated" and "amused," and "a ripple of laughter [runs] through her words" (156). She and her mother had been "his girls" (159), cherished and loved.

A little girl's loss of such a father must certainly have been traumatic and would indeed help to explain how an eighteen-year-old woman could come under the influence of her college professor. Priscilla Kiernan did not remarry after her husband's death, and so had failed to provide her daughter with another father figure. Consequently, during a time of need Nancy found her own replacement, someone she thought could guide her through the exciting but frightening challenges of her new life in college, someone who could support her developing sense of self. Carl

Harmon, whose position gave him the power and authority to teach and to evaluate, became that replacement.

As her professor, however, Carl wields his power over Nancy, his powerless pupil, forbidding her to date other men and ordering her to take her "vitamins." In effect, his actions represent the traditional power relationship between the sexes. As a man, he has more experience of the world than a woman and thus knows what is best for her. As a man, he has the duty to protect a woman, even from herself. As a woman, Nancy is expected to obey this powerful male authority. She is expected to be "good." And because Nancy has been taught to value "goodness," she complies with his demands. The constant refrain of Nancy's drug-induced exploration of the past is, in fact, "goodness." Nancy keeps repeating the fact that Carl "was so good to me," and she associates his "goodness" with the fact that "he took care of me," that "he took care of everything" (163). Nancy, however, is the "good" one in the novel. When she submits to the demands of a man whose position commands respect and obedience, she becomes the "good girl" society expects her to be. In her efforts to please, Nancy even goes so far as to become her husband's good "little girl" (159; 171). Eventually, she will encourage her own children, Peter and Lisa, to be "good" as well (164). "Goodness," however, makes victims of them all, for it denies them their own power and authority. In addition, caring, as practiced by the men in the novel, is virtually synonymous with control.

Carl's brand of "care," for instance, is clearly a type of malevolent tyranny. Yet even as practiced by Jonathan Knowles, the intelligent and kindly lawyer who rushes to Nancy's assistance, caring can be a kind of benevolent tyranny, as Clark makes clear. One of the subplots in *Where Are the Children?* involves Jonathan's increasing attraction to Dorothy Prentiss, Ray's secretary. Despite the pleasure he takes in Dorothy's company, Jonathan, a widower, is virtually "unprepared for reacting on a personal level to a terribly independent woman" (52). Reflecting upon his marriage to Emily, he admits that "an essential part of his relationship with [her] had been his constant awareness of her need for him. She never could unscrew the cap from a jar or find her car keys or balance her checking account. He had basked in his role as the indulgent, able, constant fixer, doer, solver" (248).

Jonathan's "role," however, was based on a falsehood and depended on Emily's own willingness to perform the part he needed her to play. In other words, he could only take care of his wife if he denied "the steel shaft of strength at the core of Emily's femininity" (248). Ultimately, it is just such denials that prevent women from developing independence and achieving authority. It is just such denials that create Nancy Harmon Eldredge, the victim.

As the plot of *Where Are the Children?* unfolds, however, Nancy demonstrates that she does indeed possess the inner strength of being and purpose that characterizes Emily, Dorothy, and all the other women in the novel. The seed of that strength germinated when she had, for a time, stopped taking Carl's vitamins and conceived her plan to save herself and her children from his cruel kindness. It sprouted during the six years she had been Nancy Eldredge, and it bloomed the day she faced the man who had tried to deny her being. As Lendon Miles observes of Nancy at the end of the novel: "It was a miracle that she'd had the toughness to survive the horror of everything that had happened to her. But she was a strong person and would emerge from this last ordeal, able to look forward to a normal life" (286–287).

Nancy Eldredge's struggle with Carl Harmon includes all of these interpretations as well as others, and this breadth of vision provides one of the many satisfactions of *Where Are the Children?* In her first suspense novel, then, Mary Higgins Clark endows a "good read" with something more than a breathtaking plot. By exploring the complexities of her heroine's character, she defines the nature of selfhood.

# 4

# *A Stranger Is Watching*
## (1978)

In 1976, when the U.S. Supreme Court reviewed a previous decision, *Furman vs. Georgia* (1972), and issued a new ruling, *Gregg vs. Georgia*, that effectively reinstated the death penalty, Mary Higgins Clark discovered a subject for her second novel, *A Stranger Is Watching*. Amid public protest against a cruel and unusual form of punishment and the opposition's triumphant promises of a decrease in crime, Clark added her voice to the debate.

Clark uses the elements of the suspense genre to deliver a powerful statement about the complex social issue of capital punishment. Her first novel, *Where Are the Children?*, left its topical issue, pedophilia, largely unexplored. In *A Stranger Is Watching*, however, the issue of capital punishment becomes a driving element of the plot and a central focus of the relationship between the main characters. The result is a novel of suspense with a political purpose.

The brutal murder of Nina Peterson two years prior to the events in the novel sets in motion the plot of *A Stranger Is Watching*. Nineteen-year-old Ronald Thompson now sits on death row awaiting execution for the crime. As the date of the execution approaches, Steve Peterson, devastated by the loss of his wife and raging for revenge, finds that his support of capital punishment puts him at odds with the woman he now loves. Sharon Martin, a syndicated columnist and author of *The Crime of Capital Punishment*, wants nothing more than to ease the hurt and pain of Steve and his six-year-old son Neil. She is troubled, however, by Steve's position and convinced that a terrible injustice is about to take place, and she is right. Somewhere in New York City, the stranger who murdered Nina Peterson is now plotting to kill again. His intended victim is Neil, the traumatized witness to his mother's slaying; his inadvertent victim is Sharon. When the killer abducts and holds them ransom in Grand Central Station on the eve of Thompson's execution, Steve Peterson is forced to reconsider his beliefs during his desperate search for the truth that will save them all.

## NARRATIVE STRATEGIES TO CREATE MYSTERY AND SUSPENSE: PLOT, TIME, AND SETTING

### Plot

The novel of suspense, as explained in Chapter 2, places its protagonist, or central character, in a series of threatening situations. To create and maintain suspense in *A Stranger Is Watching*, Clark employs some of the same strategies she used so effectively in her first novel. The various threads of the plot, for instance, are so skillfully interwoven that the design of the whole only gradually becomes clear. In Chapter 6, for example, the killer steals a car in Carley, Connecticut, and drives to Steve Peterson's home. Eventually, his action will connect the events related in chapters as distant as 11, 22, and 45. Similarly, a relatively minor character, a bag lady named Lolly who considers the killer's hideout her secret retreat, heightens the thrill of the chase in Chapters 13, 25, 31, 39, 42, and 49. Clark knows that one clue can enhance the whole, so she works each into her design at appropriate intervals, just in time to keep the suspense from lagging.

### Time

Clark also uses the constraints of time to great effect in *A Stranger Is Watching*. The action begins just two days before the execution of a young man readers know to be innocent. All legal appeals have been exhausted, and the governor, feeling the heat of political pressure and public outrage, refuses to intervene in the case. Ronald Thompson's fate is thus bound inextricably to that of Sharon and Neil, and time is running out for all of them.

To complicate matters, the killer has rigged a bomb to the door of his hideout, a wretched, forgotten room deep within Grand Central Station appropriately named Sing-Sing. If this prison explodes, the whole structure will collapse on itself, causing tremendous loss of life and paralyzing the city. The threat of a bomb about to explode has been used effectively by such writers as Wilkie Collins and Cornell Woolrich. The strategy works equally well for Clark, raising the level of suspense as the seconds tick away.

## Setting

Representing a cross-section of human society, Grand Central Station functions effectively as the primary setting of *A Stranger Is Watching*. Clark takes pains to render fully the life and look of this vital hub. Even after rush hour, the terminal bustles with activity, filled with people traveling to and from their varied destinations. Yet in spite of the crush of people—or perhaps because of it—everyone is anonymous in this ebb and flow of life. Even those who practically live in the station, the bag lady Lolly, her friend Rosie Bidwell, and others like them, are as much a part of the furnishings as the clock that dominates its central concourse. The terminal truly is the "crossroads of a million private lives" (58), a quality Clark will use to great effect. She noted in her essay "Suspense Writing," "I loved the possibility of the juxtaposition of kidnap victims bound and gagged near a ticking time bomb while overhead thousands of commuters rush through the terminal" (10).

The terminal's physical structure is described in detail. The celestial painting on its great vaulted ceiling is a mirror image, with the eastern stars in the west (*Stranger* 87), an error suggesting that the station's travelers may all be navigating by false signs. This ominous detail is enhanced by Clark's rendering of the "other world of the terminal," the world beneath it: "Here a pneumatic pump was throbbing, ventilating fans were rumbling, water was trickling across the damp floor. The silent, starved forms of beggar cats slithered in and out of the nearby tunnel under Park Avenue" (22). This other world, as this description suggests, is a hellish hole, and at its center is Sing-Sing, the killer's hideout.

Years before, the killer worked in this room, washing the mounds of greasy dishes sent down on the dumbwaiter from the Oyster Bar located directly above it. After the bar was renovated, the room was sealed off and forgotten—but not by the killer. Now the "cement room with cement walls from which thick layers of gray, moisture-repellent paint [are] hanging in jagged flaps" contains a "rickety canvas army cot" and an overturned orange crate. It also houses "an ancient, outsize pair of laundry tubs" whose dripping faucets "had streaked their insides with canals of rust through thick layers of caked dirt." A dumbwaiter, "entombed" by "uneven, tightly nailed boards," rises in the middle of the room. A "grimy toilet" sits inside a "dark cubbyhole" (23, 24, 301). Clark's description of her captives' prison emphasizes its repulsiveness and thereby conveys its point: Something is rotten at the core of this world, and everyone is contaminated by it.

## THEMATIC DEVELOPMENT

This rottenness functions thematically in the novel. It is, in fact, a symbol, or sign, that evokes the issues of crime and punishment that lie at the center of *A Stranger Is Watching*. The first and most obvious source of that rottenness is crime itself, and especially murder, with its implicit statement about the cheapness of human life. A second source is punishment, and especially capital punishment, which makes murderers of us all. These are the thematic issues around which all of the novel's elements swirl.

The abduction of and search for Sharon Martin and Neil Peterson set in motion the immediate plot of the novel. Yet the murder of Nina Peterson two years before—in fact, a whole series of murders in Carley, Connecticut—is truly the focus of *A Stranger Is Watching*. A serial murderer, dubbed the "C. B. Killer," is preying on the women who live in this quiet suburban community. Stranded motorists all of them, they fall victim to the good samaritan who offers to change a tire or jump start the engine. Although Nina's murder appears to be unrelated, it is really another in the series that made victims of Mrs. Ambrose and Barbara Callahan, Jean Carfolli and Mrs. Weiss, and, more than likely, other unknown women.

The crimes against these innocent victims are in themselves horrifying. They are made even more gruesome by the killer's delight in their terror and his ability to evoke it. In the moments before he kills them, the murderer records their desperate pleas for mercy. He also snaps photos of his victims, capturing forever the "twisted, screaming" mouth of one fleeing woman and the "puzzled detachment" (86) in the eyes of another.

He decorates the walls of Sing-Sing with these trophies not only to evoke paralyzing fear in Sharon, but also to savor his handiwork. This man kills for the pleasure of killing, for the feeling of utter power that arises from his actions. Other human life is without value to such a person. The resolution of the plot and the tone of the novel, however, clearly contradict this view.

When the killer dies, a victim of his own plot, Clark clearly indicates that justice has been done. A person who preys on the innocent, including a child, is undeserving of sympathy. To further emphasize her point, Clark develops her readers' concern for one of the minor characters, the bag lady Lolly. In Grand Central Station, this unknown schoolteacher from Nebraska has found acceptance of her eccentricities and, rather surprisingly, the companionship of friends for the first time in her sixty-two years. Within weeks of her arrival in New York City, she discovered Sing-Sing, the deserted room beneath the bustling terminal, and appropriated it for her private haven. Now, drawn by some inner need, some intuition to seek the shelter of Sing-Sing, Lolly becomes another innocent victim of the killer.

Alert and observant, Lolly suspects that the stranger who now frequents the terminal has discovered her retreat. She has been unsuccessful, however, in several attempts to elude the guards and investigate. Finally, convinced of the truth of her suspicions, she descends into the depths of the terminal and rushes headlong to her death. With the door to her haven in sight, the killer knifes Lolly in the back.

On one level, Clark uses Lolly to move the plot forward; because she has a key to Sing-Sing, there is always the possibility that she will use it and thereby disclose the truth. Yet the degree to which Clark focuses on this minor character suggests her thematic importance as well. Lolly's murder evokes shock and outrage because she is so undeserving of her fate. Her poverty, her anonymity, her eccentricities do nothing to diminish her humanity. Even the life—and death—of a bag lady has meaning in Clark's novel.

No matter what the cause or who the victim, crime, Clark makes clear, is unacceptable, and it demands punishment. The nature of that punishment, however, is subject to debate. Shortly after the publication of her novel, Clark articulated her views on the subject. After conducting extensive research on the death penalty, she concluded that it was morally unjustifiable. Clark is a realist, however, and acknowledges that "some of the people who commit the crimes deserve [life imprisonment] and should not be returned to society" (Stoll 20). In fact, Clark believes that some criminals do not deserve parole. "Anybody who deprives a person of life," she told Jeffrey E. Stoll, "should also be deprived of a substantial part of his own life so that he can't go out and get a beer, go to a movie or travel" (20). *A Stranger Is Watching* dramatizes Clark's perspectives on these issues.

If ever a criminal deserved to die, Clark's killer is that man, and die he does—not at the hands of a vengeful state, but by his own devices. There is justice in such a death, justice that speaks to a belief in an order and a harmony that support human existence. Would that same sense of justice prevail if the killer had been executed by the state? In the example of Ronald Thompson and the resolution of the conflict between Steve and Sharon, Clark gives her answer.

One of the most convincing arguments against capital punishment is the possibility of error, of putting to death an innocent person like Ronald Thompson. The offer of a job painting the Peterson home placed him in the wrong place at the wrong time, and now he is scheduled to die for a crime he did not commit. Despite all of the evidence pointing to his guilt, human error will cost him his life. Clark uses Thompson's situation to force her readers to confront their deepest fears about capital punishment.

Clark is not content to present only the easiest of arguments against the death penalty. She raises as well the more difficult moral issues and complex societal aspects of the controversy, using the conflict between Steve and Sharon as the vehicle for exploration.

Years before his wife Nina was brutally strangled in their home by an intruder, Steve Peterson, the editor of *Events* magazine, formed his opinion on capital punishment. In order "to preserve the most fundamental right of human beings," Steve explains, the "freedom to come and go without fear, [the] freedom to feel sanctuary in our homes," we must be willing to render unto criminals "the same harsh judgment they mete out to their victims" (67). Articulate, intelligent, and fair, Steve is a persuasive advocate for all victims and potential victims of crime, for the vast majority of ordinary citizens, in other words. His is a viewpoint shared by that majority.

Sharon Martin, despite her deepening love for Steve, has emerged as his most vocal adversary on the issue. She understands that criminals are frequently victims, too—created by the conditions of society and "tragic family backgrounds" (7). More powerful than this view, however, is her passionate belief that "the death penalty is senseless and brutalizing." During the *Today* show interview with which the novel begins, Sharon challenges her audience, and Steve, with her belief that "it is our reverence for life, *all* life, that is the final test of us as individuals and as a society" (9). Her argument also strikes a chord in readers, and thus Clark establishes the complexity of the issue.

The issue is so complex and so charged with emotion that it threatens to destroy the relationship of Steve and Sharon, who represent its inherent conflicts. It does not, however, because Steve learns a profound lesson during his ordeal, the same lesson that Clark seeks to teach her readers: nobody has the right to play God. Late in the novel, Steve confesses to reporters that he has changed his opinion about the death penalty. "I have learned," he says, "that no man has the right to determine the time of death of one of his fellow human beings" (330). Steve's change of heart and mind resolves any conflicts and unites two competing voices into one strong authorial voice. That voice speaks clearly the words of the French philosopher Montaigne: "The horror of one man killing another makes me fear the horror of killing him" (36).

## CHARACTER DEVELOPMENT

Clark is so intent on developing the central theme of *A Stranger Is Watching* that she subordinates character development to it, accounting for the major weakness of the novel. Steve and Sharon are too much the representatives of opposing viewpoints on capital punishment to be fully realized characters. Certainly Clark provides them with a history and creates a plausible life for each. Yet external realities do not necessarily explain inner being. They do not, in other words, explain the source of Steve's and Sharon's deeply held beliefs about capital punishment, nor do they convincingly explain Steve's shift in perspective. Granted, the abduction of his son and the threat that he will lose him forever do make Steve understand the pain of Ronald Thompson's mother (290). Those same events, however, coupled with the murder of Nina and the abduction of Sharon, might more easily justify a desire for vengeance on Steve's part that would lead to a hardening of his views. Similarly, her own ordeal might easily explain a shift in Sharon's views about capital punishment, but such a shift never occurs. Because Clark does not fully explore her characters' inner realities, Steve's reversal of opinion and Sharon's steadfastness occur because they must if the author is to make her point.

Clark explores the mind of a killer in more convincing detail in *A*

*Stranger Is Watching*. The man who calls himself Foxy is indeed crazy like a fox. He is also the embodiment of the Wexford curse, an ancient superstition about a fox that brings sorrow to the people who inhabit the house in which it chooses to nest (255). He gives substance, in other words, to all the deepest fears that haunt Steve's mind. What motivates him to cause such pain and to take such perverse pleasure in doing so? Clark provides two possible explanations.

Like the psychopathic killer of *Where Are the Children?*, Arthur Rommel Taggart, the "Desert Fox" of this novel, harbors a profound hatred of women. Remembering an episode in his life, an outing to Jones Beach "to meet girls" (7), Foxy exposes both his need and his inability to establish any connection to women and the pain he suffers from their rejection. From that failure and that pain is born his hatred. If he cannot woo and win women, he will possess them through cunning and stealth. For Foxy, women are the prey. Killing them confirms his ability to have what he desires.

Murder, however, is not enough for Foxy. He wants recognition as well, and this need lies behind his plan to destroy Grand Central Station. In addition to the pain of rejection, Foxy harbors the humiliation of invisibility. As a young man, he washed dishes at the Oyster Bar, "his hands all swollen from irritating detergents and scalding water and heavy wet towels." As he toiled, he was acutely aware that "all through the terminal well-dressed people had been rushing home to their expensive houses and cars, or sitting in the restaurant eating the shrimp and clams and oysters and bass and snapper he'd had to scrape off their plates, never caring about him at all." Made to feel his insignificance, Foxy is now determined to prove it a lie. The destruction of Grand Central Station, the site of so many injustices against him, will, Foxy thinks, "make everyone . . . *in the world* notice him" (24–25). Such recognition will confirm his sense of self.

## A MARXIST READING OF *A STRANGER IS WATCHING*

Clark's characterization of Foxy and her examination of crime and punishment lead inevitably to consideration of the society depicted in *A Stranger Is Watching*, especially for the Marxist critic. Such a critic focuses on the relation between literature and history, emphasizing particularly the social and economic factors that, according to the philosopher Karl Marx, drive historical change. Like feminism, with which it shares certain basic principles, Marxism is not a single theory. In fact, several different schools of Marxist critics exist, and "all of them," according to Arthur Asa Berger, "base their criticism on varying and sometimes conflicting interpretations of Marx's theories and how they can be applied to analyzing culture in general and, more specifically, literary texts, works of elite culture, popular culture, and the mass media" (41). To understand Marxist criticism, then, we need first to explain briefly the concepts which serve as its foundation.

Marx is usually classified as a "dialectical materialist." He believed that historical transformations occur through a dialectic, or development, through the stages of thesis, antithesis, and synthesis. Each historical force, according to Marx, calls into being its Other so that the two opposing forces negate each other and eventually give rise to a third force which transcends its opposition. Unlike his great teacher Hegel, who was an idealist, Marx was a materialist who believed that social forces shape human consciousness.

For Marx, the ultimate moving force of human history is economics, or perhaps more specifically, political economy. This term encompasses political and social issues as well as economic factors. Each society, according to Marx, bases its culture upon its means of production, the techniques by which it produces food, clothing, shelter, and other necessities of life, and the social relations these methods create. For example, an economy based on manufacturing demands a division of labor, cooperation among workers, and a hierarchical system of managers. These economic demands in turn shape the social relations of the people. From this basic premise, Marx argued that major historical changes occur as a result of economic contradictions, what might be termed class consciousness and class conflict. Conflict between the aristocracy and the middle classes, for example, was the source of the French Revolution of the 1790s.

In Marxist thought, the economic base gives rise to and shapes the superstructure, which finds expression in the culture's ideology, its collective consciousness of itself. This ideology is made up of all the institutions of the society, such as the church, the education system, the art world, and the legal system. Generally, the ideology, which includes literature, conforms to and supports the culture's dominant means of production. Economic conditions alone, however, are not sufficient to explain the development and effect of its institutions. Human agency, or individual consciousness, is active in these institutions as well. Thus, Marxist criticism that focuses exclusively on economics and that celebrates the proletariat, or working class, has been termed "vulgar Marxism" for its crude tendency to oversimplify complex issues.

Marxism is primarily a political and economic philosophy, not a guide to understanding literature. As a result, Marxist criticism takes a variety of forms, depending upon how the text is defined in relation to material reality or to ideology.

Clark's presentation of crime and punishment in *A Stranger Is Watching* lends itself most readily to a Marxist critique based upon the reflection theory. As an imitation of the culture that helped to produce it, the novel dramatizes the forces, both psychological and social, that lie behind criminal behavior. It also examines the political and economic forces that determine punishment. A significant aspect of them all is class consciousness and class conflict.

Grand Central Station, for instance, functions as a microcosm or miniature world in the novel, and its various levels give clear evidence of a division in society. Those with the means to pass freely through the terminal inhabit its upper regions, its great concourse and busy platforms. For them, the terminal is merely a crossroads on their journey. For others, however, the terminal is a destination. This group of people, the dispossessed, and perhaps disillusioned, wander its upper regions or inhabit its lower regions in relative invisibility, ignored by those around them. Lacking the means to proceed on their life's journey, they become prisoners along the passage.

Steve's suburban life offers additional evidence of these class divisions. Although Steve has earned his success, it was never really in doubt, given his middle-class background and his good education. He is a product of the world in which he now lives—solid, respectable, and affluent. This comfortable world, however, depends upon the toil of those like Marina Vogler. A woman pinched by the cost of living, she bemoans the fact that her car is stolen (by Foxy, of course) *after* four hundred dollars' worth of repairs that she could not afford. The suburban world of Carley, Connecticut, clearly has its own class structure, one that is no less divisive than that of the urban landscape.

Such distinct social classes, according to Marxist critics, result inevitably in class conflict. *A Stranger Is Watching* provides evidence to support this view. Foxy's rage and his disregard of others can be seen as a consequence of being ignored by others. Far below the pleasing world of the Oyster Bar he toiled in a hellish hole. Forlorn and forgotten, he made that upper world possible. The daily humiliations he suffered in his obscurity were no less hurtful for being unintended. Is it any wonder, then, that those given such a life would lash out at people who misuse or ignore them? Even a decent woman like Marina Vogler feels justified in keeping the antique moonstone ring she finds in her car as payment for her victimization. It isn't hard to see, then, how Foxy is in some ways a victim of societal inequities, a creation of class conflict.

Such a view, while it does not condone crime, complicates the issue surrounding the death penalty by linking punishment to the question of justice. Is it fair to condemn to death the criminal whose life has never really given him or her the opportunity to thrive? This is the question Kathy Moore, an assistant prosecutor assigned to juvenile court, poses to Bob Kurner, Ronald Thompson's lawyer, when she describes for him the disturbing case of one of her young clients. A fourteen-year-old boy who looks three years younger, he has already spent half of his life in and out of children's homes because his alcoholic parents have been unwilling or unable to meet his needs. Committed again to a juvenile home, the boy had run from the courtroom, hysterical and screaming, "I hate everybody. Why can't I have a home like other kids?" (131). Kathy knows that it is already too late to save him. In five or six years he will probably come before the judge having killed someone, and she wonders, "Will we burn him? Should we?" (132). The answers to her questions are far more complex than the crime itself might suggest.

Clark's emphasis on class conflict evokes another question of justice, one she articulates most clearly in an interview with Jeffrey E. Stoll: Is it fair to condemn to death the criminal who lacks the money to avoid capital punishment? As Clark tells Stoll, "The death penalty is rarely applied fairly. There's a saying that nobody who makes $50,000 a year is ever executed." In fact, according to Clark, those most commonly executed are "usually pretty pathetic individuals" (Stoll 20). Ronald Thompson is certainly proof of Clark's statement. The young man fresh out of high school who bags groceries and stocks shelves for a living is doomed before he goes to trial. The cost of justice is high, too high for the majority of ordinary citizens.

By examining the social and economic factors that give rise to crime, Clark gives some truth to the Marxist critique of hierarchical societies. She offers as well yet another argument against capital punishment. Whatever the critical stance, however, this issue lies at the center of the novel. *A Stranger Is Watching* succeeds as a novel of suspense, but it does more than that. It challenges its readers to think hard about the world in which they live, a world full of the defeated and the dispossessed, some of whom turn to crime. It asks them to consider the nature of justice and the intent of punishment. But finally, as Steve Peterson's reversal of opinion clearly indicates, it demands that we acknowledge what Mary Higgins Clark sees as the truth about capital punishment—that it diminishes us all.

# 5

# *The Cradle Will Fall*
## (1980)

With the publication of her third novel, *The Cradle Will Fall*, Mary Higgins Clark explored the territory of another mystery suspense writer, Robin Cook. There, in the sterile corridors of a respected suburban hospital, she found all the ingredients necessary to create her own medical thriller. Written in the aftermath of the birth in England of Louise Brown, the first "test-tube" baby, *The Cradle Will Fall* raises many of the legal and ethical issues surrounding that birth by focusing particularly on the plight of vulnerable women desperate for children who become victims of a ruthless doctor. The novel demonstrates once again Clark's ability to produce gripping suspense from the headlines. It illustrates as well her continued interest in the hopes and fears that motivate our lives, for in her focus on the crucial relationship between doctor and patient, Clark explores the devastating consequences of a betrayal of trust.

In *The Cradle Will Fall*, Kathleen DeMaio, a prosecutor in a small New Jersey town and the young widow of a judge, is briefly hospitalized following a minor auto accident. That night, from her window, Katie sees a man loading a woman's body into the trunk of a car. Heavily sedated, she thinks she has had a nightmare until she begins investigating the suicide of her sister's pregnant neighbor, Vangie Lewis. When the suicide begins to look more like murder, Katie realizes that it was Vangie's face she saw in her vision. Although initial evidence points elsewhere, Dr. Richard Carroll, the medical examiner, soon establishes a trail to Dr. Edgar Highley, a distinguished gynecologist and reproductive specialist whose "Westlake Maternity Concept" has produced miracle babies for infertile couples. As more deaths follow, Katie tries to convince herself and others of what she saw, and Richard gathers evidence against Dr. Highley. Before Richard can warn Katie, however, she enters Westlake Hospital for minor surgery with Highley, who had seen her at the window on that fateful night. Now, Highley is determined to eliminate this witness against him.

## NARRATIVE STRATEGIES TO CREATE MYSTERY AND SUSPENSE

Suspense rather than detection drives the plot of *The Cradle Will Fall*, for readers know almost from the beginning the identity of the criminal. They know as well his plan to murder Katie DeMaio, Clark's engaging heroine. Much of the suspense, therefore, turns on whether or not he will successfully accomplish his mission. Clark creates, in other words, the classic suspense situation, as explained in Chapter 2.

The novel's suspense depends as well upon Clark's skillful handling of time and place. Clark's choice of the hospital setting, for instance, feeds into the deep-seated fear of death and dying that many people, including Katie DeMaio, associate with the sights, sounds, and smells of that mysterious place. The chill of its sterile corridors, the odor of its antiseptic atmosphere, the controlled panic in its "code blues" are enough to evoke dread in the most confident of patients as well as their visitors. They are constant reminders of the secret practices going on behind its closed doors. To enter a hospital is to face mortality, to experience vulnerability, to surrender control. Katie DeMaio certainly understands this dread. It has, in fact, caused her to delay medical treatment. However irrational her fear may be, though, Katie shares it with countless readers of the novel, and Clark draws upon it for her novel's atmospheric tone.

Identification with Katie DeMaio also enhances Clark's handling of the novel's time element. The accident that sends Katie to the hospital, making her a witness to murder, occurs less than a week before the surgery that is intended to end her life. During that short time Katie proves herself a competent professional, a compassionate woman, and a genuine human being undeserving of the fate that Dr. Highley has planned for her. Nevertheless, she rushes blindly toward it, hastening it, in fact, by her refusal to confide in Richard. By giving her readers the knowledge that Richard must solve one crime in order to avert another and making them aware of the inevitable passage of time, especially when Katie is bleeding to death, Clark drives them relentlessly toward the novel's terrifying climax. They simply must know that Katie DeMaio survives.

Clark recognized Katie's role in achieving the novel's suspense. In her essay "Suspense Writing," she confesses that she had written fifty pages of *The Cradle Will Fall* when she realized that the novel had a "fundamental flaw": "I couldn't get worried about Katie." As the wife of a superior court judge, Katie would be loved and protected. Clark "just knew that when John DeMaio got home the next day, he'd make very sure that no one would hurt his Katie." The solution to the problem was to make Katie the widow, not the wife, of the judge. "Immediately," Clark realized, "she is infinitely more sympathetic—vulnerable and alone in the large secluded house she inherited from him" ("Suspense Writing" 12). The change also had the advantage of adding a love interest to the tale. From such stuff did Clark build her novel's suspense.

## CHARACTER DEVELOPMENT

The protagonist of *The Cradle Will Fall*, twenty-eight-year-old Katie DeMaio, is certainly worthy of the reader's concern, and thus she is a character around whom to create suspense. She is also essential to the development of Clark's thematic issues (as are most of the novel's other characters). A competent prosecutor who has earned the respect of her colleagues, Katie genuinely cares about the work she does because she is convinced that her success vindicates the victims of crime. The auto accident that sends her to Westlake Hospital, in fact, results because "the intense satisfaction of the guilty verdict [she had just won] was still absorbing her" (1). Katie brings this same intensity and commitment to all her cases, including the investigation of Vangie Lewis' "suicide."

Katie's professional success, however, is not a sufficient compensation for her personal unhappiness. Granted, she is surrounded by a loving family and shares a comforting relationship with her sister, Molly Kennedy. Nevertheless, Katie still feels her essential "aloneness" (3). She was still grieving for the adored father who died when she was eight years old when she met and married Judge John DeMaio, twelve years her senior. A friend and lover, he was determined "to uproot that core of sadness" (23) in her, and he had nearly succeeded. A diagnosis of cancer shortly after their honeymoon, however, turned their marriage into a deathwatch and abruptly widowed Katie.

During her brief marriage, Katie moved into the house John had been raised in and had inherited from his parents (22), and "in those few short months, in every way, they had become one" (24). John's death thus leaves Katie feeling utterly abandoned, inwardly raging, and despite appearances to the contrary, unable to move forward in her life. She refuses to sell the house she shared with John, and she resists the advances of, and her own attraction to, Richard Carroll, the county medical examiner. Instead, Katie directs her anger and grief into her work. In the prosecution of crime, she believes that she is "tangibly fighting at least one kind of evil that destroyed lives" (25).

Katie's essential vulnerability is at least part of her charm as a character, for it contributes to her believability. It humanizes this competent professional woman, making her someone with whom readers can identify. More important, however, her vulnerability and its source contribute to the development of one of the novel's secondary themes—the uncertainty of life.

The untimely deaths of both the men she has loved—her father and her husband—have caused Katie to fear life. Indeed, for Katie, the fact of death robs life of its promise. All her plans with John were devoured by the cancer that killed him. Now, whereas the other women in the novel are focused on creating new life, Katie clings to the past, living on her memories of John, something permanent and secure.

Katie's brush with death, however, helps her to accept life's uncertainties. As her life's blood flows from her body, Katie, for all intents and purposes, dies. Yet death, as she discovers, is as uncertain as life. Something pulls her back from finality. Perhaps the same instinct that causes her to resist death prompts her to risk life, for all life, as she discovers, involves risk. Joan Moore, for instance, is willing to risk her reputation to save Chris Lewis, the man she loves. Vangie Lewis and Liz Berkeley are willing to risk their lives to bear a child. Dr. Highley is willing to risk murder to achieve a medical miracle and thereby to secure his reputation. Katie, however, has been willing to risk very little, finding it better to live with the pain she knows than the anguish or joy that lies in the unknown future. When Katie cheats death, then, she learns an important lesson about life, a lesson that Clark clearly endorses.

Equally important to the success of *The Cradle Will Fall* is Edgar Highley, Clark's particularly insidious villain and the embodiment of "one kind of evil" that Katie fights. Having corrupted his genius, Dr. Highley is about to reap the rewards. The publication of a magazine article praising the Westlake Maternity Concept as a miracle treatment for infertility will make him famous. The treatment, however, is fraudulent, based on unethical and medically dangerous experimentation on unsuspecting women desperate to bear children. When Vangie Lewis, one of his experiments, threatens to expose him, Dr. Highley murders her.

Like Marlowe's Faustus, Mary Shelley's Frankenstein, and Nathaniel Hawthorne's Chillingworth, Clark's Dr. Highley thinks highly of his genius. And like them, he is the man of genius gone wrong. Dr. Frankenstein used his scientific knowledge to create life and thereby achieve godlike power. His creation, however, was a physically and mentally deformed monster that made a mockery of its creator. Hawthorne's Chillingworth promises to aid the Reverend Arthur Dimmesdale, the guilty lover of Hester Prynne in *The Scarlet Letter*. Chillingworth uses his position, however, to prey upon his patient and thereby punish him. His cold-blooded calculations against Dimmesdale assert his intellectual superiority, but they expose his moral failings.

Similarly, Dr. Highley enjoys his reputation and believes that his innate superiority entirely justifies his violation of others. If he must sacrifice a Vangie Lewis, so be it. He has already sacrificed two wives to his infernal treatment. The murders of those who threaten him now— Edna Burns, his secretary; Dr. Emmet Salem, a former colleague who knows his past; and Katie DeMaio—are or will be inconsequential in the larger scheme of things.

No matter how he justifies his actions, Dr. Highley is nothing more than a cold-blooded killer, and Clark takes care to prevent readers from developing any sympathy for him. The death of his mother in childbirth, willingly risking her life to bear him, may have motivated Dr. Highley to begin his research. He has long since lost sight, however, of his original intention. Now this ego-driven man enjoys gourmet dinners following his evil deeds. After the murder of Dr. Salem, for instance, Highley feeds his sense of well-being by dining on "smoked salmon, vichyssoise, a rack of lamb" (202) in the quiet elegance of the Carlyle Hotel. Highley's insatiable appetite is Clark's metaphor for utter depravity. He feels not a pang of remorse for his victims.

## THEMATIC DEVELOPMENT

Clark's portrayal of the physician corrupted gives substance to the primary theme of *The Cradle Will Fall*, the devastating consequences of trust betrayed. Clark signals her thematic intention when she quotes Hippocrates, the Greek physician who is considered the father of medicine, as the novel's preface: " . . . for some patients, though conscious that their condition is perilous, recover their health simply through their contentment with the goodness of the physician." Hippocrates' words give special weight to the relationship between good health and the good physician, clearly suggesting that the one is dependent upon the other. He asserts as well the crucial importance of "contentment," the peace of mind that derives from absolute trust, in the healing process.

Equally important in Hippocrates' observation is the word "goodness," for its several meanings create the whole. On the one hand, goodness suggests competency. The good physician, by virtue of his or her knowledge of the human body, is skilled in the art of healing. He or she can treat illness, cut out disease, mend parts, and thereby restore the patient to health. On the other hand, goodness also implies virtue. The good physician, by virtue of his character, commits his skill to the healing arts. He or she takes the Hippocratic oath, pledging to uphold the highest ethical standards, and thereby gains the trust of the patient. Such trust is, according to Hippocrates, equally essential to the restoration of health.

Given this context, Edgar Highley is the worst sort of villain. In betraying the trust of his patients, he robs them of their well-being; he steals from them their physical being or their emotional life. Dr. Highley's murder victims give silent but damning testimony of this point. Equally persuasive, however, are his other victims, those who bear the scars of his experiments. Clark provides two such witnesses in *The Cradle Will Fall*.

Maureen Crowley, the efficient young secretary in the prosecutor's office, still nurses the wounds that Dr. Highley inflicted when he "treated" her. Young and unmarried, Maureen had just broken her engagement to her high school sweetheart when she realized that she was pregnant and sought a solution at Westlake Hospital. Now, several years later, Maureen is wracked by guilt about the abortion Dr. Highley forced her to have.

Similarly, Anna Horan, the young wife of a law student, is consumed by rage following her "treatment" by Dr. Highley. The sole support of her family, Anna concluded that she must have an abortion when she discovered she was pregnant. On the day of the procedure, however, as she sat on the operating table, Anna changed her mind. In spite of her efforts to resist, Dr. Highley, after injecting her with a powerful sedative, performed the abortion.

Both women were unsuspecting victims of Dr. Highley's conceit and his unethical experimentation. Both were emotionally shattered because they had placed their trust in a physician who ignored his obligations. The consequences of this betrayal of trust, however, ripple far beyond Maureen and Anna, touching two other women as well.

Dr. Highley's unethical and dangerous experimentation involves implanting aborted fetuses in the wombs of sterile women. Maureen Crowley and Anna Horan have been Highley's unwilling donors; Liz Berkeley and Vangie Lewis have been his unsuspecting hosts. Their wombs have become the cradles for Maureen's and Anna's fetuses. Liz, "a Carol Burnett type" (194), gives birth to a "fair-complexioned, red-blond [daughter], with brilliant green eyes" (198). Her "daughter" is, of course, the image of her biological mother, Maureen. Vangie, however, has been implanted with the fetus of Anna Horan, a Japanese woman, and genetic incompatibility threatened her life. It was also unexpectedly threatening to expose Highley's treachery, and when the bough broke, the cradle did indeed fall. Vangie and Anna's unborn child died because Highley "became so fascinated by his own research that he couldn't bear to destroy the fetus" (311–312). As Richard Carroll later discovers, sixteen other women had previously been sacrificed to Dr. Highley's experiments.

The allusion, or indirect reference, in the novel's title to the traditional lullaby helps to convey Clark's primary theme. A baby snug in a cradle is still endangered when that cradle rests upon the bough of a tree. A gentle wind may rock the cradle, but a fierce storm can sever the limb from the trunk. And "when the bough breaks, the cradle will fall," sending both the cradle and its precious contents, the baby, to their ruin. The allusion to the lullaby suggests, then, that the cradle, or woman's womb, as Dr. Highley refers to it (155), is threatened by the very person who seems to support it—Highley himself. His betrayal of all that is humane and good in the healing arts is the ill wind that destroys all.

## A FEMINIST READING OF *THE CRADLE WILL FALL*

The subject of *The Cradle Will Fall* invites a feminist interpretation because it clearly raises some of the fundamental issues (more fully explained in Chapter 3) underlying the gender differences and gender expectations on which such critics focus. Many feminist critics, for instance, explore the degree to which gender is a biological construct. They ask, in other words, to what degree women are defined by their bodies.

Clark's answer is not one that would please most feminists, for the women in *The Cradle Will Fall* seem to have nothing in common except baby longing.

So desperate to bear children are Liz Berkeley, Vangie Lewis, and Dr. Highley's other unnamed victims that they are willing to submit their bodies to any sort of treatment, no matter how experimental or potentially dangerous. Liz Berkeley even undermines the trust on which her marriage is based to become a mother. Her husband, Jim, had refused to consider conception through artificial insemination (246–247). Following the birth of their daughter, however, he suspects that Liz has deceived him. He knows that it is highly improbable that their red-blond cherub is genetically related to either of her dark "parents" and feels betrayed by his wife's perceived dishonesty. Clearly, in their efforts to give birth, these women confirm the view that they are incomplete without children. While men secure their reputations by their accomplishments, women, as these characters testify, must fulfill their biological function—they must give birth and become mothers—if they are to achieve their full potential.

Molly Kennedy, Katie's supportive sister, reinforces this perspective in the novel. The happily married mother of six children, Molly can simultaneously nurse a sick child, chase away Katie's blues, and whip up a batch of tempting Reubens. She is the complete nurturer, even to her younger sister, for whom Molly's house is "a haven of normality" (37) after the grim realities Katie faces on her job. Molly functions in this novel as an ideal of womanhood: She is mistress of her domestic world and utterly fulfilled by it. She has and is what every other woman in the novel needs and seeks to be.

Even Katie DeMaio, the competent professional woman, feels the pull of Molly's example. Returning to the "serene peace" of her own home following a visit to the Kennedys, for instance, she feels "the emptiness of her house and [tries] to imagine what it would be like if John were still alive and their children had started to arrive" (37). Later, following the surgery necessary to save her life, Katie's first concern is for her ability to bear children. When Katie seeks the answer "she had to know" (313), Richard assures her that she "can still have a dozen kids if [she wants] them" (313). Katie's destiny, like that of every woman, Clark's novel seems to say, is to fulfill the traditional roles of wife and especially mother.

This view of a biological destiny, however, is certainly problematic, for it reduces women to their reproductive function and thereby diminishes their humanity. The risks that the women in *The Cradle Will Fall* are willing to take to bear children obviously indicate the degree to which they have themselves accepted this view. The novel's most chilling expression of it, however, resides in Dr. Highley. Here is a man who refers to "the womb as a cradle" (155). He believes that "the place to eliminate [birth defects] is not in the laboratory, but in the womb" (154). Eventually, his emphasis on the womb rather than the woman leads him to his dangerous experimentation. For someone who speaks of body parts as if they were disconnected from the person, the transplantation of one woman's embryo into the womb of another woman is simply good science. It is also the logical extension of belief in biological destiny. The humanity of the specimens is simply not part of the equation.

Dr. Highley's monstrous experimentation and his obvious literary antecedent in Dr. Frankenstein also connect the novel to feminist readings of Mary Shelley's classic tale. Like Dr. Frankenstein, Highley enacts the birth myth, creating life through his science and from his intellect and thereby becoming like Eve, the first mother. But Dr. Highley's creation is the genetically incompatible fetus that was killing Vangie Lewis, just as Victor Frankenstein's is a vile and degraded monster that kills its creator. Both creations symbolize the moral deformity of Eve. In eating of the forbidden fruit, she gives birth to sin and death. She causes the expulsion from Eden; thus, by implication, woman is the source of humanity's suffering. Woman, in other words, gives birth to the deformed. Dr. Highley's connection to Dr. Frankenstein thus exposes his monstrous experimentation as an expression of his own deep hatred of women.

This feminist perspective on *The Cradle Will Fall* echoes and expands Clark's primary theme, reinforcing her point about the sanctity of the individual. When a doctor transforms his patients into specimens, he or she exposes them to dis-ease. When the members of one sex are reduced to their biological parts, they are valued only for their biological function. When one person murders another, he or she demonstrates a contempt for life. Every one of these cases, Clark's novel indicates, constitutes a crime against the individual, indeed, against all humanity. Every one of these cases is the consequence of a betrayal of human relationships, a failure to enact our human obligations to others. These are the poignant and powerful truths of *The Cradle Will Fall*.

# 6

# *A Cry in the Night*
## (1982)

Dreams of Prince Charming are common for most little girls, but they are not unusual for their adult selves either. Nurtured on the tales of Cinderella and Sleeping Beauty, young women sometimes find themselves longing for a perfect man who will rescue them from their ordinary lives. He will, of course, be handsome, but more important, he will be sensitive to their needs and strong enough to shoulder the burdens of life. When he finds them, their lives will be wondrously changed, and they will, of course, live happily ever after.

The fairy tale of desire fulfilled is the basis of Mary Higgins Clark's fourth best-seller, *A Cry in the Night*. When Erich Krueger, a newly discovered artist from the Midwest, sweeps Jenny MacPartland, a struggling young divorcée and mother of two daughters, into marriage, he is her dream come true. Prince Charming has indeed rescued Cinderella from poverty and privation. But fairy tales take place in the world of "Once upon a time," not in Greenwich Village or even on an idyllic family farm in Minnesota, especially if Mary Higgins Clark is telling the tale. In *A Cry in the Night*, Clark rewrites the traditional fairy tale and thereby creates a gripping novel of mystery and suspense that exposes the tale as a lie. In doing so, she also gives her readers a heroine who learns an important lesson about self-reliance and self-fulfillment.

Jenny MacPartland's marriage to Erich Krueger one month after the twenty-seven-year-old divorcée meets the art world's newest discovery sets in motion the plot of *A Cry in the Night*. Until he entered her life, the plucky mother of two toddlers had been struggling to support them. Suddenly, however, she finds herself the wealthy wife of a man who adores both her and her daughters, a man who intends to care for them always. Jenny can hardly believe her luck. Transplanted from their Greenwich Village apartment to Erich's vast Minnesota farm, Jenny is eager to create a warm, caring home and to join the life of the community. Erich, however, cannot bear to share her with others, nor can he tolerate change in his family farm. He also disappears for days at a time to paint at his secret studio. Lonely days evolve into eerie nights, and Jenny, her nerves strained to the breaking point, soon begins to doubt her sanity. When Kevin, Jenny's feckless ex-husband, drowns under suspicious circumstances and her newborn son mysteriously dies, Jenny becomes a murder suspect. Yet this is the least of her troubles. Erich has abducted her daughters and threatens to keep them forever. How Jenny saves herself and her daughters from a haunted present, a living past, makes for a terrifying tale of suspense.

## GENERIC CONVENTIONS

With its vulnerable yet resourceful heroine and its endangered children, *A Cry in the Night* bears the hallmarks of a Mary Higgins Clark novel of suspense (outlined in Chapter 2). Yet it also charts movement into new territory for her. Unlike her previous novels, *A Cry in the Night* relies as much upon mystery as suspense to achieve its effect. Her early works used an omniscient narrator, capable of revealing the thoughts, dreams, and feelings of the characters as well as events in the past, present, and even the future. From this all-knowing perspective, Clark took readers into the mind of the criminal and thereby revealed his or her identity almost from the outset of the tale. This strategy heightened suspense by providing readers with more information than the endangered heroine possessed. Yet it also eliminated the "whodunit" element from the plot. Given that crucial information, readers raced to the novel's end to determine how the heroine escaped the cruel fate that awaited her, not to solve the mystery.

In *A Cry in the Night*, however, Clark withholds vital information from her readers so that they learn the truth with the heroine. She limits herself to the heroine's point of view (the perspective from which we see and understand the characters and events) and in doing so lends an element of mystery to her tale. Readers are convinced that Erich is the source of all the strange events in Jenny's life, but they do not know how or why he is manipulating the situation. They know as well that the death of Erich's mother years before is a key to the mystery. Like Jenny, however, they do not possess that key and are thus unable to unlock the door to the truth. The result of Clark's narrative strategy is to create an eerie atmosphere reminiscent of the gothic tradition in which this novel is rooted.

In the outlines of its plot, *A Cry in the Night* resembles Daphne du Maurier's *Rebecca* and Charlotte Brontë's *Jane Eyre*, two classics of the gothic tradition. These novels of terror and suspense focus on a young woman alone in the world. The unnamed heroine of du Maurier's novel marries an older man of sophistication and wealth without really knowing him. Swept away to the de Winter estate, Manderley, she soon falls victim to her own insecurities and the psychological terror engendered by the ghostly presence of her husband's former wife, whose accidental drowning haunts everyone in the household. Jane Eyre, an orphan, takes a position as governess at Thornfield Hall, the ancestral home of Mr. Rochester, and soon falls in love with her employer. She, too, experiences the terror of locked rooms, haunted corridors, and mysterious cries in the night. In their sinister and claustrophobic environments, both women even begin to distrust the men they love, whose brooding silences and unexplained absences do little to reassure them. At the heart of these novels is a mystery—a madwoman in the attic, an unusual drowning— knowledge of which empowers the heroine to confront her own demons and thereby save herself.

The novel's setting also links *A Cry in the Night* to tales of gothic suspense. Although Erich's farm is neither decaying nor gloomy, it is inhabited by the presence of others, specifically his mother, Caroline. The rooms have been preserved just as they were when she died nearly twenty years before, and the scent of the pine soap she loved still pervades the atmosphere. In addition, Erich's boyhood room sits unchanged at the end of the hall, still inhabited by his adult self. Jenny feels little more than a visitor in Erich's ancestral home, especially when she realizes that she may do nothing to alter it. When she rearranges the furniture and removes heavy curtains and personal bric-a-brac, for example, Erich works late into the night to restore his home to its original condition. For him, it must forever bear the stamp that Caroline placed upon it.

Within this place, the merely strange gradually becomes the menacing.

First, cakes of Caroline's soap mysteriously appear on the children's pillows. Then Jenny awakens in the middle of the night with the sensation that someone is watching her from behind her bed; when she reaches up her arms, she touches—or thinks she touches—a face. Secret passages and haunted rooms are the stuff of the gothic romance, and Erich's farmstead serves as a modern equivalent to the medieval castle or manor house. It inspires the same terror in its heroine that those traditional settings inspired in theirs. For Jenny, this place becomes not a refuge, but a prison.

## THE GOTHIC TRADITION IN THE DEVELOPMENT OF CHARACTER

The characterization in *A Cry in the Night* also recalls the gothic tradition. Jenny MacPartland is a worthy counterpart to the heroines of other gothic tales. Typically, she is an orphan. In fact, she is doubly orphaned, first by the automobile accident that killed her parents when she was a toddler, and then by the recent death of the beloved grandmother who raised her. When she meets Erich Krueger, she is at a particularly vulnerable point in her life. The loss of her grandmother as well as her divorce from Kevin, an aspiring actor, has robbed her of financial stability and emotional support. She is struggling to meet the demands of her job in a Manhattan art gallery and motherhood. So when Erich enters her life, Jenny is delighted to have someone with whom to share her responsibilities, someone to relieve her loneliness. For all her need of Erich, however, Jenny possesses a quiet strength upon which she draws in a crisis. Intelligent and forthright, she also brings a realistic attitude to life. These are the qualities that link Jenny to the gothic heroine.

In fact, Clark takes care to shape this view of Jenny in the novel's Prologue. In that sequence, Jenny wakes at dawn and listens for a baby's cry that does not come. Dressing warmly against the bitter cold of February, she sets off on skis to find her husband's cabin in the woods. One year after her marriage, Jenny is still ignorant of the location of his secret retreat. On this morning, however, she is determined to find it. Because she fears getting lost in the snow-covered blankness of unknown territory, Jenny has devised a strategy for her search. Finally, at dusk, physically and emotionally exhausted, she locates the cabin—empty and locked against her. Jenny, however, will not be deterred from her quest.

Breaking a window with a hammer, she gains entry and searches for the clues she needs to accomplish her mission. The nature of that mission is as yet a mystery to Clark's readers. What is clear to them, however, is the heroine's determination to succeed, even in the face of the horrifying evidence that she finds there. When she leaves the cabin, Jenny carries with her a painting, a hideous representation of herself, which reveals a truth she has been seeking.

The Prologue establishes the tone of both mystery and suspense essential to the success of *A Cry in the Night*. Even more important, however, it establishes the character of Jenny MacPartland and makes her a credible heroine. Clark's strategy here is crucial, for in the flashback that follows this episode, Jenny is in danger of becoming too much the victim. Generous to a fault, she continues to "loan" money to her irresponsible ex-husband Kevin despite her own meager salary. Eager to please, she quickly agrees to Erich's proposal to adopt her two daughters. When the new family moves to Minnesota, Jenny takes virtually nothing from the past with her. She is beginning a new life, and her trust in Erich is virtually absolute.

For much of the novel, Jenny's virtues are reduced to faults, especially her desire to please. On their wedding night, for instance, Jenny agrees to wear the gown that had belonged to Erich's mother instead of her own choice, even though she feels uncomfortable doing so. Similarly, when Erich restores the farmhouse to its original decor, rebuffing her efforts to make it her own, Jenny silently acquiesces to avoid confrontation. Even when she learns that her husband has been withholding her mail and her telephone calls, even when he refuses her the keys to the car, Jenny says nothing to him. Time after time Jenny submits her will to Erich's in order to please him.

Such innocence, such vulnerability, although characteristic of the gothic heroine, have the potential to undermine the reader's belief in Jenny's ability to save herself and her daughters from the man who possesses them. Yet that same reader cannot forget his or her initial impression of Clark's heroine, where Jenny demonstrates her resourcefulness, her strength of purpose, and her good sense. Readers never doubt that such a woman will prevail.

Clark's use of this narrative strategy to develop her heroine's character also serves to undermine the connection between Jenny and her double in the novel, Caroline Krueger. In literature, a double is a character who resembles or duplicates the characteristics of another or who shares similar experiences with another. A ghostly presence every bit as pervasive as Daphne du Maurier's Rebecca, Caroline exerts a powerful influence on the lives of Jenny and Erich. In fact, her story threatens to become Jenny's story, so closely are the two characters related.

Jenny bears an uncanny physical resemblance to Caroline, and that resemblance immediately draws Erich to the young woman. Like Jenny, Caroline had come to the Krueger farm as a young bride. On her arrival, she had been encouraged by her husband to abandon her considerable talent for painting and to channel her artistic sensibility into the more acceptable female occupations of homemaking and quilting. Caroline had gradually begun to suffer the same loss of self that Jenny experienced, and like Jenny, she had also attempted to flee her prison. On the day of her appointed escape, however, Caroline had died in what everyone believes was a tragic accident. Her efforts to save herself—and to save her child, who had, she feared, become overly attached to her— came too late. She was prevented from making her escape, in fact, by the same person who now plots to destroy Jenny. Despite their resemblance, however, Jenny is not Caroline, nor is she living Caroline's story. Her fate, as the Prologue suggests, will differ from Caroline's because Jenny is capable of writing a different ending to her own story. She will not rely upon a hero or a Prince Charming to do it for her.

If Jenny is the traditional gothic heroine, Erich Krueger fulfills the role of gothic hero only superficially. Certainly he is handsome, charming, intelligent, and sensitive, and given to brooding silences and mysterious disappearances. He promises to rescue the heroine from an impoverished life and thereby ensure that she lives happily ever after. And in time the heroine begins to doubt and fear him. In the gothic romance, however, the heroine's doubts are eventually proved false. The hero is indeed the Prince Charming of fairy tales. But in the world of Mary Higgins Clark the hero is the villain. Erich Krueger is a deeply disturbed man who does indeed threaten to destroy Jenny MacPartland.

From the moment Erich meets the woman who bears a striking resemblance to his beloved mother, the woman who gives life to memory, he is determined to possess her, and within a month he does. During their whirlwind courtship, he is a solicitous lover and a doting father, and is almost able to conceal the ruthlessness that lies beneath his pleasing exterior. That ruthless streak surfaces, however, at least for the reader, in his efforts to adopt Jenny's daughters. He will have what he wants and has the money to buy it if necessary. His gifts to Jenny may indeed be a sign of his generosity, but they also effectively sever her ties to her old life. With their new clothes, purchased with Erich's money, they have become what he wishes them to be—his.

Any doubts about Erich's intentions are dispelled by his next actions. He prevents Jenny from receiving telephone calls, claiming that he must guard the solitude he needs to be creative. When she learns that he has also been withholding her mail, however, Jenny feels the menace in his acts. On several occasions Jenny catches her husband in lies and suspects that he is isolating her from any community. Consequently, when he forbids her the use of the car, Jenny understands that she has virtually become his prisoner. She cannot believe his seemingly loving explanations for his actions and feels his concern as cruelty. These actions pale in comparison, however, to Erich's cruel acts: the abduction of Jenny's daughters, the murder of Jenny's former husband, and the killing of his own newborn son. All of these acts make plausible a ten-year-old boy's murder of the mother he believed had betrayed and abandoned him. This is the secret that lies deeply buried at the heart of *A Cry in the Night*. This is the secret that reveals the true nature of Erich Krueger. It is certainly no hero that Jenny must confront at the novel's end.

## THEME

The lessons of Jenny's brief but tragic marriage to Erich Krueger are certainly not lost on Clark's readers. In fact, they spell out fully the central theme of *A Cry in the Night*: To place one's happiness in the hands of another is to risk all. Eager to believe that the man of her dreams will make her "happily ever after" come true, Jenny is willing to ignore the disturbing and disquieting to preserve her dream. Yet Jenny eventually discovers that in doing so she has abdicated control of her very existence to someone with his own vision of her future.

Faced with the truth about her husband, Jenny relies upon her wit and her courage to defeat his perverse plot against her. She makes those treacherous forays into the Minnesota blankness to search for Erich's cabin alone. She pieces together the meaning of Erich's paintings. She devises her own plan to lure Erich to his doom and is willing to risk her life to save her daughters. Ultimately, Jenny's refusal to be a victim allows her to reclaim her life and to forge another, but on her own terms. When she determines to donate the Krueger farmstead to the local historical society, Jenny steps out of the haunted past and into an uncertain future, but she is clearly capable of meeting its challenges. She now controls her own destiny.

Moreover, Jenny will not make the same mistakes again, as Clark's treatment of her relationship with Mark Garrett makes clear. For most of the novel, Garrett, Erich's closest friend since boyhood, is a quietly reassuring presence in the background of Jenny's life. During the darkest days of her ordeal, however, he steps forward to support the woman to whom he is clearly attracted, and she allows him to assist her. Gradually, Jenny responds to his unassuming strength and his undemanding friendship, but she does not rely upon it. By the novel's end, she and Mark share the promise of a relationship, but nothing more. Unlike other Clark novels, *A Cry in the Night* does not conclude with the heroine resting safe in the arms of the man who loves her. Rather, it ends with its heroine planting her garden, sowing the seeds of new beginnings. Mark Garrett remains quietly in the background, part of that promise. Yet he is no Prince Charming—because Jenny wants no such hero. By leaving this relationship unresolved, Clark thus reinforces her novel's central theme.

## A PSYCHOLOGICAL READING OF *A CRY IN THE NIGHT*

*A Cry in the Night* is a novel whose meaning expands when different critical perspectives are focused on it. A psychological interpretation of Erich Krueger's character, for example, might apply the strategies of Freudian and Jungian psychology to explain motivation and actions in clinical terms.

For the purpose of understanding *A Cry in the Night*, aspects of both Freudian and Jungian psychology can help to explain the conduct of the novel's tormented antagonist. As the antagonist, Erich Krueger is the character who stands in opposition to the novel's protagonist, or central character, Jenny MacPartland, and is thereby the source of the conflict in the plot. To explain his behavior, Freudians would point to Erich's conflicted feelings for his mother as evidence of an unresolved Oedipus complex. According to Freud, every child experiences latent sexual feelings toward the parent of the opposite sex. He named these complex feelings for Oedipus, who in fulfillment of an oracle kills his father and marries his mother in the ancient Greek tragedy by Sophocles, *Oedipus Rex*. Freud theorized that these feelings were initially positive, but if they were unresolved, they could be the source of adult personality disorder.

In other words, the child must eventually suppress his or her sexual attraction to the parent of the opposite sex and identify with the parent of the same sex to become a fully unified adult. Failure to achieve this transfer of affection and identity leads inevitably to psychological turmoil in adulthood.

Given this perspective, Erich Krueger's is a classic case of the unresolved Oedipus complex. *Memory of Caroline*, for instance, the painting that Erich keeps with him always, is clearly a representation of his mind. He is haunted by the mother he loved to obsession, the mother he killed to possess, and his relationship with Jenny is merely an extension of that other relationship. Jenny's initial attraction for Erich, for example, is her uncanny resemblance to Caroline. In his mind, she becomes Caroline, and thus his marriage to Jenny is a union with his mother. In fact, he can only make love to Jenny when she wears the aquamarine satin nightgown that had been Caroline's.

Emotionally stunted, Erich is still the ten-year-old boy who felt so abandoned and betrayed by his mother that he murdered her to prevent her leaving him and his father. His childhood bedroom has been preserved intact. It is, as Jenny realizes on her first night in her new home, "frozen in time, as though growth in this house had stopped with Caroline's death" (65). Even after his marriage, Erich continues to sleep in his childhood bedroom. It offers him a return to the innocence of childhood and helps him to deny the complex emotions of adulthood, those forbidden emotions that make of his mother an object of desire. From a Freudian perspective, then, unresolved feelings, including sexual feelings, for his mother explain Erich's obsessions and actions.

Jungian psychologists would also find in Erich's relationship with his mother the source of his subsequent actions. They believe that the Anima, the female principle that resides within the unconscious mind of every man, is affected, if not shaped, by his mother. According to Jung, the Self comprises four aspects. On the surface is the Mask, or the face we show to the world. Beneath it lies the Shadow, a demonic image of evil that we tend to reject or keep hidden from consciousness. The Anima represents the female element found in all males; the Animus represents the male element found in all females. Because the Anima is shaped by the man's mother, it may be either a dark or light force within the unconscious. Consequently, it may lead to either well-developed, unified personalities or to disturbed ones. If the mother's influence is positive, the Anima reinforces a man's sense of masculinity and helps him to explore his inner values. If the mother's influence is negative, the

Anima aspects of the man's personality will be dark and will result in harmful consequences.

From this perspective, Erich's actions are evidence of a deeply disturbed Anima and of the disastrous effect Caroline's intended departure had on her son even into adulthood. For a ten-year-old boy, that departure had nothing to do with saving herself and her son and everything to do with cruel abandonment. Shaped by this view, Erich's image of women thus focused on deception and betrayal, and these qualities constituted his archetype of woman. When he marries Jenny, Erich projects this image onto her, so her actions and motives are always suspect to him. Her desire to have the car keys, for instance, looks to Erich like an intent to abandon him rather than a bid for freedom of movement. Similarly, her request to meet others looks to Erich like a denial of his central place in her life rather than an effort to connect to her new community. Because he sees his distorted image of woman in Jenny, Erich cannot see her as she truly is, nor can he trust her love and devotion. In effect, then, his distorted image of woman explains Erich's obsessions and accounts for his destruction of his marriage.

## A FEMINIST PERSPECTIVE ON *A CRY IN THE NIGHT*

A feminist reading of *A Cry in the Night* would approach the literary text from the perspective of gender differences and gender expectations (see Chapter 3 for a fuller explanation). In doing so, feminist critics would focus particularly on the novel's ending and the way in which Clark overturns traditional narrative structures. They would seek, in other words, to understand Clark's reasons for using certain accepted and expected elements of plot development, in this instance, those related to the fairy tale, but then altering them for her own purposes.

The stories that shape the views of women are traditionally the fairy tales of Prince Charming upon which they are nurtured as young girls. Generally, these tales teach the importance of a man to a woman's physical and emotional well-being. This man will save her from a life of hardship and unhappiness if she submits to his benevolent love and guidance, symbolized in their marital union. Even the gothic hero, dark and mysterious though he may be, ultimately proves to be a figure from romance. His flaws transformed as his secrets are revealed, he is thus another version of the idealized male.

When Clark evokes the fairy tale and the gothic romance through her characters and her novel's structure, she raises in her readers certain expectations about the ending. Jenny and Erich are to some extent stereotypical characters. They both conform, in other words, to a fixed or typical pattern that readers should recognize. They also participate in a traditional drama. Their tale should, then, end in "happily ever after." When it does not, readers experience a certain amount of unease. That unease, however, is healthy, feminists would say, healthier, in fact, than the comfortable pleasure produced by the romantic ending, which is restrictive and unrealistic. It denies the heroine the power to shape her own life and promises the impossible. Clark's ending, in contrast, is liberating. Jenny's recognition of the tyranny of Erich's kindness and concern gives her the power to act, and when she does, she assumes responsibility for her own happiness and achieves it. When Clark overturns the traditional romantic ending, she teaches her readers a different lesson, a lifesaving lesson, one that undermines entirely the false truths of those other stories.

These additional perspectives on *A Cry in the Night* eventually bring readers back to Clark's central theme, lending it depth, breadth, and reinforcement. Equally important, they demonstrate as well Clark's ability to make a conventional literary form and a popular genre something more than an entertainment. Ultimately, *A Cry in the Night* is the perfect remedy to counteract the traditional messages of its genre, and her cautionary tale is all the more powerful because Clark uses the genre to challenge itself.

# 7

# *Stillwatch*
## (1984)

---

Political intrigue provides the background for intrigues of another and deeper kind in Mary Higgins Clark's fifth novel, *Stillwatch*. The intersecting stories of two successful professional women drawn together by the dark secrets in their pasts allow Clark to explore once again some familiar territory. Specifically, she reexamines the nature of identity and the process of self-definition. Yet her skill as a storyteller makes it seem as if she is venturing into uncharted seas. The novel is every bit as suspenseful as her previous works, but perhaps more satisfying, and the reason is clear. In *Stillwatch*, Clark achieves the perfect balance of mystery and suspense and uses both elements to demonstrate the ways in which the past touches upon the present.

Set amid the political intrigues of Washington, D.C., and the competitive world of broadcast journalism, *Stillwatch* tells the linked stories of Patricia Traymore and Abigail Jennings. The novel begins when Pat, a successful television producer, moves from Boston to the nation's capital to develop a series of profiles on intriguing people for Potomac Cable Network. She chooses as her first subject Senator Abigail Jennings, a woman on the verge of political triumph. Abigail hopes to be named vice-president of the United States following the impending resignation of the ailing man who holds the office. Her nomination is not, however, a certainty, for she faces stiff competition from the equally capable but more personable Senator Claire Lawrence. To improve her chances, Abigail reluctantly agrees to cooperate with Pat, who greatly admires her subject. In fact, she hopes to produce a profile that will humanize the senator, going beneath the cool exterior to the warm human being she feels sure is there. As Pat delves into the past, however, she learns of facts that could destroy Abigail. At the same time, those same facts could save Pat, for she has her own personal motives for coming to Washington. She has returned to her childhood home, the scene of a terrible crime never fully explained, to uncover the secrets that lie deep within her memory. Those secrets unexpectedly involve Abigail. Someone, however, is determined to prevent Pat from producing her feature, determined enough to kill her if necessary. What begins, then, as a quest for the truth suddenly becomes a matter of life and death.

## NARRATIVE STRATEGIES TO CREATE MYSTERY AND SUSPENSE: TIME AND POINT OF VIEW

### Time

Clark relies upon some of her standard narrative strategies, such as her handling of time, to create the suspense of *Stillwatch*. The events in the novel occur during a period of one week, Christmas week, in fact, and this constriction of time adds an edge to the action. Everything becomes crucial and thus suspenseful, especially when the heroine is in danger.

Pat had planned an expansive schedule during which to produce her feature and thereby do justice to her subject. She arrives in Washington, however, to discover that time is of the essence. Everyone in the capital expects Abigail to be appointed to the vice-presidency before the year's end. If Pat is to take advantage of the situation and boost the ratings, she must prepare her profile in seven days, hardly enough time to conduct the research and shoot and edit the tape.

The drama of professional urgency is complicated, however, by Pat's knowledge that someone intends to prevent her from producing her feature. Even before arriving in Washington, she received threatening letters warning her to cease her investigations, and the threats continue to arrive as she races to complete her program. Thus, what is initially only a nearly impossible deadline becomes a matter of life and death. Moreover, the whole drama will play itself out during the Christmas holidays, as if to mock the festive season.

## Point of View

Clark's handling of point of view, the perspective from which the story is told, also heightens the suspense. Once again she places her readers within the mind of a killer. Arthur Stevens is a deeply disturbed man who believes he is an avenging angel responding to messages from God (245). A former ambulance attendant, he now works as a hospital orderly, moving from place to place when he comes under suspicion for the deaths of his patients. Such suspicions are entirely justified because Arthur, in his other role as angel of mercy, frequently hastens the deaths of the old, the infirm, and the terminally ill. Nine years before, he had befriended a young woman recovering from a nervous breakdown, and now he will do anything to protect her from harm. Pat Traymore's profile threatens to expose the true identity of the woman he calls Gloria, for as Eleanor Brown she was convicted of a theft she maintains she did not commit. By placing her readers within the mind of Arthur Stevens, Clark provides them with a unique perspective. They know who is stalking Pat and why. Thus, they become like Pat's neighbor, Lila Thatcher, a clairvoyant who knows something is wrong and determines to conduct a stillwatch, or vigil, over her. Unlike Lila, however, readers are powerless to keep Pat from harm, so their superior knowledge merely increases their own anxiety and thus the novel's suspense.

Placing her readers within the mind of Arthur Stevens also allows Clark to deepen the element of mystery surrounding Pat Traymore and her Georgetown home. Arthur had been one of the ambulance attendants called to the scene of a murder-suicide more than twenty years before. He still remembers the three-year-old girl, her leg shattered and her head bleeding, who lay crumpled like a Raggedy Ann doll against the fireplace. That little girl is now Patricia Traymore. In other words, Arthur holds some of the keys to the mystery Pat has come to solve, but she does not know it. Clark's readers do, however, and thus are given the opportunity that mystery readers love—the chance to solve the crime. As in every good mystery, however, the solution runs deeper than the clues provided by any one character. Thus, Clark's narrative strategy merely teases readers and keeps them guessing.

## CHARACTER DEVELOPMENT

If Arthur Stevens holds some clues to the mystery at the center of *Stillwatch*, Clark's two women protagonists hold all of the answers. One of them, however, has so deeply buried her memory of an event she only partially understood that she may die before her mind gives up its truths. The other woman has so hidden her involvement in the affair that she now fears the consequences of exposure. One of them is determined to uncover the secrets of the past whatever the cost. The other is equally determined to prevent the past from destroying her. Their intersecting stories and their differing attitudes toward the mysteries of the past are the heart of *Stillwatch*. They are thus the focus of Clark's character development.

On the surface, twenty-seven-year-old Patricia Traymore has everything going for her. Her previous work has already garnered Emmy nominations. Now her reputation for getting her subjects to reveal themselves with remarkable candor during an interview has given her the opportunity to produce her own series, called *Women in Government*. She is clearly riding a wave of professional success.

Beneath the surface, however, Pat is haunted by a past she can barely remember, a past that altered the course of her life in ways she can only imagine. As Kerry Adams, she had once been the darling daughter of Congressman Dean Adams and his wife Renée. Secure in the love of both parents, she had been happy in the life they shared in their Georgetown home. When she was three years old, however, her life changed in an instant. Dean and Renée, one of three popular young congressional couples that included the John Kennedys, were found dead in their living room, victims, according to the official verdict, of a murder-suicide. Their beloved daughter had sustained a serious injury to her leg and a concussion that virtually erased any memory of the tragedy that had unfolded that night. Barely clinging to life, the child had been transferred by her grandmother to a Boston hospital, and there, so far as the world knew, Kerry Adams had died. As Patricia Traymore, however, the adopted daughter of her mother's sister, Kerry Adams had lived. Now, more than twenty years after the tragedy, she has returned to Georgetown to do more than produce a television show. She has come to recover the past in response to the "bits and pieces of memory that had intruded on her like wreckage from a ship" (5) for some time. As she confesses to her new neighbor Lila Thatcher, "I need to link the child I was to the person I am" (170).

Haunted by dreams of her childhood in the Georgetown house, Pat is convinced that it holds "the truth" (5) as soon as she steps across its threshold, and her instincts are exactly right. As she busily sets up house-keeping, for instance, she realizes that she has unconsciously re-created the home of her three-year-old self (23). Furthermore, with every passing day, more and more of her suppressed memories rise to the surface. Yet the most crucial continue to elude her. Although she has entered the house of the past, which functions in this novel as a symbol of the mind, Pat simply cannot reconstruct her relationships with the parents who once shared her life there.

Indeed, it is those relationships that have been so troubling for Pat, forming the source of the "pervading sense of loss" (5) that has existed in the background of her life. She simply does not know her parents. Granted, her grandmother and adoptive mother shared with her their memories and photographs of Renée. Moreover, once she returns to the Georgetown house, she herself vaguely recalls the sensitive woman who spent long hours playing the piano in the living room. Her father, how-ever, is little more than an absence in her memory. Nobody tried to help her preserve an image of the man responsible for their family tragedy. Yet whatever she thinks she knows about her parents, the truth is con-cealed in mystery, and Pat must remove that veil if she is to reconcile the child that was with the woman that is.

Some of the keys to that mystery are packed away in the file cabinets and boxes of souvenirs and keepsakes that had been transferred from her father's congressional office to the basement of the Georgetown house following his death. Now Pat begins to mine those sources, dig-ging for the truth that eludes her. What she initially discovers surprises her, for it is a truth about herself, not her parents. Combing through the appointment books and framed diplomas, the collage of snapshots and the citations and honors, Pat uncovers evidence of more than just a dis-tinguished career. She finds as well proof of her father's generous and warm-hearted character. This unexpected discovery has a surprising effect on her, forcing her to admit her hatred for her father and "to face the anger she had been denying all these years" (52).

Pat's task is further complicated by the evidence she uncovers. Open-ing her father's appointment book, for example, she realizes from whom she acquired the habit of doodling (53). Examining family photographs, she recognizes her face in her father's, not her mother's. But the most confusing evidence is preserved in one special photo "of a tall, laughing man with a child on one shoulder" (52). The child is smiling with delight and clapping her hands in joy. This photo tells Pat that "the child she had been . . . clearly had trusted the man holding her, trusted him not to let her fall" (53). It seems impossible to her that the man in that photo could have murdered her mother and tried to murder her. It seems impossible as well to hate such a man.

Thus, in the opening chapters of *Stillwatch*, Clark reveals the troublesome undercurrents beneath Patricia Traymore's polished surface. Intelligent and sophisticated, Pat possesses an uncompromising drive to seek the truth, and that quality has helped her earn her reputation. Yet she is also an emotionally scarred survivor of violence that severed her from her parents and from herself. As the limp in her right leg symbolizes, Pat is damaged, and to repair the injury she must pursue the truth. She must separate her anger from her sadness, her illusions from reality, to free herself from the past.

Clark's other protagonist in *Stillwatch* provides a sharp contrast to Pat, for Abigail Jennings fears her past and wants nothing to do with it. In fact, she seems to have invented herself as she is—a United States senator. Granted, she has a past, but only a public one as the young widow of a prominent senator whose term she completed following his death in an airplane crash and whose seat she subsequently won on her own. Although during her political career she has developed a reputation for workaholism and made powerful enemies on her climb to the top, she has the skill and savvy to make things happen in Washington. Now she is about to reap the rewards of success. She may not be as popular with the public as Senator Claire Lawrence, but everyone in the capital believes Abigail will soon be appointed vice-president.

The past that Abigail has worked so hard to bury begins to surface when Pat makes her the subject of the first *Women in Government* feature. Hoping to "give viewers the feeling of knowing her on a personal level" (16), Pat believes she has discovered Abigail's secrets. Her life of poverty, hardship, and humiliation in upstate New York, for instance, was far different from the privileged Virginia background that she has allowed others to believe was hers. In addition, she had once rejected the Miss New York State beauty crown for a Radcliffe scholarship. Moreover, the thirty-one-year-old widow had never found another man to take her husband's place and is still unmarried twenty-five years after his death. These are the details of a life that will evoke a television audience's sympathy for another human being, Pat is convinced. So Abigail reluctantly agrees to cooperate with the project, even though she fears that Pat will discover that there is more to these details than she suspects.

What Pat learns does indeed lead her to the underside of Abigail's secrets and to a reevaluation of her character. When a picture of Abigail as Miss Apple Junction is published in a national tabloid, for instance, the senator is ashamed because her mother is overweight. The Radcliffe scholarship also becomes suspect when Jeremy Saunders, Abigail's former fiancé, tells Pat that it was a bribe to her from his family to end their relationship. Even Abigail's tragic widowhood is tainted by allegations that the airplane crash that killed her husband may not have been an accident and that their marriage was far from perfect. The Abigail who begins to emerge from Pat's investigations is a bundle of contradictions. A passionate advocate for her constituents and an effective legislator she most certainly is. But Pat also begins to believe that Abigail has lied and schemed her way to the top, that her polished surface disguises ruthlessness and lack of principle rather than compassion and high ideals.

Abigail's dark underside has always been visible in the shape of her "oxlike chauffeur" (30), Toby Gorgone. Drawn together by mutual need and unhappiness during their teenage years in Apple Junction, Toby and Abigail share a "bizarre relationship" (30) understood only by themselves. Rumor has it, however, that they will do anything to serve and protect each other. Pat's investigations give her reason to believe the truth of those rumors. Eleanor Brown, Arthur Stevens' Glory, may have been sacrificed by Abigail to conceal Toby's embezzlement of her campaign funds. Congressman Sam Kingsley, the man Pat loves, also begins to suspect that Toby, a mechanical genius, may have been involved in the plane crash that killed Willard Jennings. Whatever the truth of the rumors, however, it is clear that Toby is Abigail's dark alter ego, or second self. In fact, his surname, Gorgone, evokes the three snake-haired sisters of Greek mythology, the Gorgons, whose glance turns the beholder to stone. As her alter ego, Toby instinctively understands Abigail's needs and enacts some of her most desperate wishes. In fact, he eliminates many of the obstacles to her goals without ever having to be asked to do so.

The parallel lives of Clark's two protagonists begin to intersect when Pat uncovers one other surprising element of Abigail Jennings' past— her close friendship with Dean and Renée Adams. During their brief ascendancy in Washington, the Adamses had been part of a popular trio

of congressional couples that included the Willard Jenningses and the
John Kennedys. Abigail had frequently been a guest in Adams' Georgetown home. Yet there may have been more to the friendship than others
know. When she attends the glamorous Christmas party of one of her
politically powerful neighbors, for example, Pat overhears gossip about
her parents. Some believed that they were planning to divorce. Others
claimed that her mother was deeply disturbed and insanely jealous and
that her father had a reputation as a womanizer. Then, when newspapers
publish a photo that unmistakably captures an intimacy between her
father and Abigail, Pat begins to question her memories of the tragedy.
She wonders as well about Abigail's involvement in it. Eventually she
learns that Abigail knew more about her parents' deaths than anyone
had suspected. In fact, what Abigail knew but did not tell is enough to
ruin her political career.

## THEMATIC ISSUES

The relationship between Pat and Abigail is more complex than the
solution to this mystery suggests. In fact, it is central to the thematic
concerns of *Stillwatch*. At its most basic, *Stillwatch* is, as Clark has said
in an interview, a novel about "two women's relationship to their past"
(*Loves Music* n.p.). As such, it develops a frequent Clark theme—the presence of the past in the here and now. Although her heroines have opposing attitudes toward the past, each of them learns the same lesson.
Like a stone dropped into a still pond, the past creates a ripple effect
that stretches into the present moment. It touches the lives of even the
unsuspecting, but it may have the power to change the course of the
lives of those closest to the event. The murder-suicide of Dean and Renée
Adams, for example, set in motion a chain of events that played itself
out more than twenty years after it had faded from the memories of
most people. Until it reached its end, however, it touched the lives not
only of those who knew them, but also of those who knew someone who
knew them, such as Catherine Graney and Eleanor Brown. Even these
strangers could thus become innocent victims of circumstance.

Moreover, as the events in *Stillwatch* suggest, efforts to conceal, deny,
or escape the past are ultimately fruitless and may even be harmful.
Eleanor Brown, the campaign worker falsely convicted of theft, runs
from her past and creates a new life and a new self as Glory. Yet her
new existence has never brought her peace. Fearing exposure and living

always under a cloud of self-imposed suspicion, Eleanor finally determines that she must surrender to authorities and face her past if she is to have any sort of life.

Similarly, Abigail Jennings topples from the pinnacle of success not because she was Miss Apple Junction, but because she attempted to hide that part of her past, as if it were cause for shame. She falls not because she was involved in the Adams tragedy, but because she refuses to admit her involvement. Abigail's crimes are almost exclusively sins of omission rather than commission. In every case, however, they leave her vulnerable to exposure and ruin. Ultimately, Abigail's efforts to conceal the past are little more than an admission of its presence in and power over her life, which is exactly Clark's point.

The relationship between Pat and Abigail also permits Clark to explore relatively new thematic territory for her. In *Stillwatch*, she examines the degree to which we create our reality, which encompasses the past, from our own psychological need. Once she learns the circumstances surrounding her childhood, for instance, Pat, aided by her grandmother's and adoptive mother's versions of the past, creates a fiction to live by. According to this story, Dean Adams is the cold-blooded murderer of a loving wife. Renée Adams is a sensitive and artistic woman who shared her talents with an adoring daughter. All the blame for hurt and loss falls on the father who betrayed them all.

Digging into her past, however, forces Pat to separate truth from illusion. The father she had cast as a villain and the mother she had viewed as a victim are humanized by her recognition of their joint failures and their individual strengths. As bits and pieces of the past begin to surface in her memory and connect to make a coherent whole, Pat admits, "I have so many preconceived ideas—my mother was an angel, my father a devil" (171). This admission helps Pat to strip away her illusions and to find the truth that restores both her parents and her past to her and allows her to embrace the legacy of self bequeathed to her by both. When she can once again be the child of both Dean and Renée Adams, Pat is finally able to acknowledge her identity to the world and to move forward in life. At the novel's end, when Sam asks Pat about her feelings toward her parents, she can honestly reply, "Happy that it wasn't my father who pulled the trigger. Sorry for my mother. Glad that neither one of them hurt me that night. They were absolutely wrong for each other, but so much that happened was nobody's fault. Maybe I'm starting to understand people better" (355–356). Pat's response is certainly a measure of her own increased maturity.

This humanizing of her parents occurs simultaneously with the humanizing of Abigail Jennings, for in many ways Pat stands in relationship to her as she had to her mother. To some extent, in fact, Abigail has been a surrogate mother for Pat, the model of the successful professional woman that Pat hopes to be. From the beginning, Pat's choice of Abigail for her first profile has as much to do with hero worship as it does with her *Women in Government* series. Her "growing obsession to do a program about Senator Jennings" stems from her great admiration of the other woman's accomplishments. She also holds a deep conviction that "Abigail Jennings should lead the ticket" (14) in the next presidential election. Frequently, Pat waxes eloquent about Abigail to Sam Kingsley (14). She also argues vehemently with Abigail for her own concept following the publication of the Miss Apple Junction photograph (187). In every case, her actions and beliefs clearly reveal her idealization of the senator. It is the idealization of a daughter for a mother, a student for a teacher.

Yet just as Pat's exploration of the past reveals her mother's failures and flaws, so, too, does it expose the human side of Abigail Jennings. As Pat gradually comes to realize, the public Abigail is indeed different from the private Abigail, and neither is quite what Pat had conceived her to be. Indeed, Pat's view of Abigail is perhaps more a creation of her own need for a role model than a realistic assessment of a fellow human being. Abigail's accusation—"You *like* Cinderella stories" (187)—speaks directly to Pat's tendency to idealize. Yet her own project to humanize Abigail forces Pat to admit her role model's flaws and to learn one of the other lessons of *Stillwatch.*

## A FEMINIST READING OF *STILLWATCH*

*Stillwatch* provides Clark with another opportunity for some rather insightful cultural criticism. Just as in *A Stranger Is Watching*, Clark turns her attention in this novel to a controversial social issue, the sexual double standard. Such a critique is based on the feminist theory outlined in Chapter 3 and concerns itself primarily with issues of power and gender. Feminism investigates not only the realm of literature, but sociological, economic, and political ideas as well. Thus, it invites readers to consider the ways in which gender issues are reflected in the text, especially if we view the world of the novel as a representation or recreation of its society. From such a perspective, we may consider the treatment of women in professions traditionally controlled by men. That treatment, as Clark portrays it in *Stillwatch*, is blatantly sexist, both demeaning and unjust to women.

Pat Traymore, for instance, is a model of the serious professional woman of the post–Equal Rights Amendment (ERA) era. Bright and articulate, capable and self-confident, she has earned professional recognition for her work as well as the promotion that brings her to Potomac Cable Network. Sexually liberated, Pat also actively pursues the man she loves. In fact, she refuses to allow him to treat her like a child (11) or to ignore their mutual attraction, even if *he* wishes to deny it. Yet for all her success and self-confidence, Pat is a victim of sexual harassment.

Shortly after she assumes her position at Potomac Cable Network, Pat attends a meeting with her boss, Luther Pelham. He is "both pleased and annoyed" by this woman who seems so "totally at ease" that she is unafraid to examine him. He also admits to himself that "he had found himself doing a lot of thinking about her in the two weeks since he'd offered her the job." He notes specifically "a smoldering sexiness about her that was especially intriguing" (46). Pelham's appreciation of Pat, however, is accompanied by resentment of her privileged social standing. The fine cut of her clothing, the designer trademarks, speak obviously of money and cause Pelham to recall the humiliations of "his own humble beginnings" (49). Before long, Pelham is acting on his ambivalence about Pat.

On the evening of Pat's return to Georgetown following her background trip to Apple Junction, Pelham invites himself to her home for a briefing. His plan, however, clearly involves something more than work. When Pelham suggests that Pat sit beside him on the couch, she ignores his invitation and chooses instead a chair separated from him by the coffee table. Yet before the evening is finished, Pelham rises, walks around the table, and embraces Pat. Then he forces his kiss upon her Pat escapes his "viselike" grip by digging her elbows into his chest. Then she bluntly tells him, "I don't sleep on the job nor do I sleep off the job. Not tonight. Not tomorrow. Not next year." Smiling cruelly, Pelham warns her, "Sometimes people who have your kind of insomnia problem find it impossible to handle their responsibilities" (85). In no uncertain terms, Luther Pelham has just humiliated Pat, who has unintentionally caused him to feel old humiliations. He has used his power to threaten her. He has, in other words, sexually harassed her.

Abigail, too, is a victim of sexual double standards. Driven by ambition, she is unafraid to pursue her goals. In fact, she has a reputation as an uncompromising legislator who "doesn't care who she blasts, and where and how she does it" (14), as Sam tells Pat. That reputation has not endeared Abigail to many of her senatorial colleagues, and yet, as Pat forces Sam to admit, the same is "also true of the majority of the men on the Hill" (15). Such conduct is accepted in a man, but in a woman it is considered unbecoming. Assertive behavior in a woman, in fact, may cause some to view her as cruel and insensitive. Abigail may lose the vice-presidential appointment, in other words, because she is too much like her male colleagues and not enough like her chief rival, grandmotherly Claire Lawrence.

Yet Abigail's Miss Apple Junction crown leaves her open to ridicule as too much the beauty queen to be taken seriously for her other talents. Moreover, the role she played as dutiful wife and helpmate to her husband has the potential to undermine the accomplishments she achieved on her own. In other words, Abigail risks losing the nomination because she is a beautiful woman who, in the minds of her critics, may have earned her rewards not for her intellect and skill but for her sex. Others will simply stand firm on traditional views that a woman lacks the ability to hold the nation's highest political office.

In focusing on the sexual politics to which her heroines fall victim, Clark exposes some of the ugly truths about contemporary culture. Despite their obvious talents and their professional successes, both Pat and Abigail find their sex to be a liability. Certainly women made gains during the (unsuccessful) drive for ratification of the Equal Rights Amendment. Nevertheless, the seats of power are filled by men who are unwilling to admit women to their clubs and unafraid to demand sexual favors of the women who work for them. Through her heroines, then, Clark prods her readers to consider the plight of ordinary women. If women of the stature of Pat and Abigail find their opportunities compromised by sexual harassment and sexual discrimination, what hope have those in lesser positions or those with lesser force of character in similar circumstances? Not quite enough, Clark suggests, and indeed, the historic moment her novel anticipated provided a disheartening footnote to her tale.

In 1984, just as *Stillwatch* was being released, Walter Mondale, the Democratic candidate for president, named Geraldine Ferraro as his running mate. As Clark remembers it, "The 1984 election was coming up. I anticipated the Democrats 'talking' a woman vice-president and decided to beat them to it" (*Loves Music* interview n.p.). As the first woman to run for this high political office, Ferraro found herself subject to unprecedented scrutiny, much of it of a kind no man would have faced. Although many voters believed the nation was ready to accept a woman's leadership, reaction to Ferraro's nomination clearly suggested otherwise. She and Mondale were soundly defeated in the November 1984 election. Ten years after the publication of *Stillwatch*, Clark's political ending—a woman vice-president—remains an unrealized dream.

Ultimately, the society that serves as the setting of *Stillwatch* provides some additional perspectives on Clark's more common themes and concerns. On both the personal and the political level, the past exerts a powerful force. Just as the lives of Pat and Abigail are shaped by the past and their responses to it, so are the institutions upon which society rests. In fact, those institutions are so firmly rooted in the past that they are deeply resistant to change. Those individuals who confront their pasts, however, find themselves capable of moving forward in life or of salvaging their existence. In *Stillwatch*, then, Clark gives new life to and expands some recurrent themes by returning to contemporary issues and thereby evoking real concerns of very real people.

# 8

# *Weep No More, My Lady*
## (1987) and
# *The Lottery Winner*
## (1994)

The glamorous world of an exclusive California health spa might seem an unlikely setting for intrigue and murder, but not in the hands of Mary Higgins Clark. In her sixth novel, *Weep No More, My Lady*, Clark assembles the five likely suspects in the murder of the actress Leila LaSalle (for which one is about to stand trial) in just such a place. There as well comes the grief-stricken sister who is determined to uncover the truth. At Cypress Point Spa, amid the kneading and pounding of pampered bodies and the gourmet cuisine of the celebrity diet, Clark then exposes the truth of the saying "Beauty is only skin deep." Elizabeth Lange's efforts to solve the mystery surrounding her sister's death will call into question the sincerity of those who professed their love and friendship for the temperamental actress. They will also force her to face their selfishness and duplicity. And they will lead her to examine the nature of her own complex relationship with the sister she had loved perhaps more than herself.

Until she plunged to her death from the balcony of her Manhattan apartment, Leila LaSalle had been one of the most famous stars of stage and screen. Adored by her fans, Leila had also been loved by her younger sister, Elizabeth Lange, an aspiring actress in her own right, and Ted Winters, the handsome president of Winters Enterprises to whom she was engaged. Around her circled a small group of trusted friends and even a personal and professional rival.

Minna von Schreiber created Leila LaSalle, and now, with her husband, the aristocratic Baron Helmut von Schreiber, she operates Cypress Point Spa. Syd Melnick was Leila's agent, and Craig Babcock, Ted's assistant, was her former lover. Dora Samuels, her personal secretary, would have done anything for Leila. Cheryl Manning, an actress who had once been involved with Ted, would have done anything to her. Now, one year after Leila's death, Ted Winters is about to be tried for the murder of his fiancée, and Elizabeth is the key prosecution witness. Convinced that Elizabeth is mistaken about what she heard on the night of the murder, Min determines (for reasons beyond mere friendship) to save Ted. She invites all the players in this drama to Cypress Point Spa, and there the final act will be staged. Before the curtain falls, everyone will betray a motive for murder, and two persons will fall victim to the desperate killer. In response to her own doubts about Ted's guilt, Elizabeth will then use herself as bait to trap the culprit. The question is whether she will survive to tell what she knows.

## NARRATIVE STRATEGIES TO CREATE MYSTERY AND SUSPENSE: TIME AND SETTING

In typical fashion, Clark creates the suspense of *Weep No More, My Lady* by placing her unsuspecting heroine in a menacing situation. Then she heightens the intensity by the press of time. Elizabeth's return from filming a movie in Italy one week before Ted Winters' trial for the murder of Leila LaSalle is scheduled to begin provides the compression of time which is a hallmark of Clark's plot development. Additionally, each section of the novel is organized around the events of one day of that week, thereby emphasizing the inexorable movement toward what seems an inevitable guilty verdict. Clark then intensifies the suspense built into this structure. She concludes each day with either an attempt on Elizabeth's life of which she is unaware, or the murder or attempted murder of another innocent victim. This compression of time gives rise to the anxiety that the novel of suspense is expected to produce in its readers.

Clark also makes effective use of setting to create a sense of mystery and menace. Although Cypress Point Spa nestles within the dramatic cliffs overlooking the pounding surf of the Monterey coastline, its most prominent natural feature, the cypress trees that dominate the grounds, gives the landscape an ominous appearance. To Syd Melnick, the cypress trees, "with their crazy twisted shapes," are a source of discomfort and psychological unease. He remembers that "some poet had compared them to ghosts" (90), and that comparison immediately evokes the ghost of Leila LaSalle, which seems to haunt them all. Elizabeth also responds to "the silhouettes of the cypress trees" one evening following an attempt on her life of which she has been unaware. Her response, however, her feeling that the trees seemed "grotesque and ominous in the dark" (172), suggests that she has somehow sensed the danger that surrounds her in this landscape.

Contributing to the haunting and foreboding atmosphere is the new Roman bath that is under construction on the manicured grounds. When Elizabeth first sees the structure, "its black marble exterior, accentuated by massive columns," reminds her of a "mausoleum" (41). This comparison proves apt; one unfortunate victim will indeed lose her life in this eerie place. Late one night, when Dora Samuels, Leila's former secretary, surprises the killer there, her backward plunge into an empty pool transforms the bath into "Sammy's sepulcher" (217). These primary natural and structural settings clearly emphasize the underside of Cypress Point Spa. In fact, they stand in sharp contrast to the subtle decor of the guest rooms and the gleaming opulence of the public rooms, both of which are intended to give the spa a patina of beauty and luxury and, by implication, respectability.

## POINT OF VIEW

*Weep No More, My Lady* is more a novel of mystery than of suspense. To keep the reader guessing "whodunit" to the end, Clark modifies at least one of her typical narrative strategies. Because the mystery is a tale of secrets revealed, the writer must provide clues to the solution of the puzzle. She must also simultaneously withhold crucial information until the detective is prepared to reveal all. In classic tales of mystery and detection, readers are seldom, if ever, given access to the criminal's mind. Nor are they permitted to enter the detective's mind. Instead, most of these stories are narrated by a participant in the events, usually the detective's assistant. They may also be related by an omniscient narrator, an objective voice who can convey the thoughts of any of the characters and who has knowledge of the past, the present, and even the future.

To provide her readers with special knowledge that enhances her novel's suspense, Clark frequently exposes them to the criminal's mind, thereby reducing the element of mystery. In *Weep No More, My Lady*, however, her handling of the criminal is guarded. A brief glimpse into that mind early in the novel establishes that Leila's murderer intends to kill Elizabeth. On several other occasions, usually following an unsuccessful attempt on Elizabeth's life, readers enter the criminal's mind to learn that he will not be deterred from his mission. In every instance, however, Clark takes care to withhold the criminal's identity as well as any obvious clues that might reveal it. Thus, she creates suspense in the typical fashion of a mystery novel. She makes readers aware of her unsuspecting heroine's endangerment, but without sacrificing the element of mystery so crucial to the novel's success.

*Weep No More, My Lady* shares many of the stylistic and narrative strategies typical of her fiction. Clark does, however, introduce some innovations into this novel, particularly in her handling of point of view. Although she has frequently taken readers into the mind of her criminal, never before has she recreated the voice of a victim and made it an essential part of her narrative. In *Weep No More, My Lady*, one of Clark's most important characters, Leila LaSalle, becomes a living presence in the novel because she speaks in Elizabeth's memories.

Rather than have Elizabeth paraphrase her sister's evaluation of Baron Helmut von Schreiber, for instance, Clark re-creates Leila's voice saying to Elizabeth, *"I swear, Sparrow, that guy makes me think of a toy soldier"* (44). And later, when Elizabeth is confused by seemingly contradictory and incomprehensible evidence, she hears Leila telling her, *"Stop seeing what people want you to see. Start listening. Think for yourself. Didn't I teach you that much?"* (314). By giving voice to the dead, Clark provides some insight into her victim's character. Readers hear her cruel characterizations and her cynical judgments, and the evidence in her own voice gives them reason to understand how such a woman could be the victim of murder. Rather than tell her readers that Leila provoked contradictory feelings in even her closest friends or that she loved her sister like a daughter, Clark dramatizes this character whose presence haunts the novel. Through her own voice, readers thereby come to know the victim.

In the character of Alvirah Meehan, Clark also experiments with a comic voice in *Weep No More, My Lady*. An unlikely guest at Cypress Point Spa, Alvirah has just won 40 million dollars in the New York State lottery. The first extravagance for this middle-aged, middle-class former cleaning woman is the Cypress Point Spa treatment. Alvirah, of course, is entirely out of her element amid the quiet elegance of the spa and among its patrons, who are accustomed to the ease of wealth. In fact,

Elizabeth is able to spot her immediately as she and the spa's chauffeur wait at the airport on the morning both women arrive. The last one off the plane, Alvirah wears a "purple-and-pink print" that does nothing to flatter her "bulky" frame. The outfit is "obviously expensive," notes Elizabeth, "but absolutely wrong for her" (30). Beyond a doubt, this woman is Alvirah Meehan.

Although Elizabeth immediately likes this unlikely client and finds her genuine honesty refreshing, the spa's other patrons are not quite so indulgent. They would be even less so if they knew that the sunburst pin everyone notices Alvirah fiddling with conceals a microphone that records their voices. Alvirah Meehan is taping their conversations without their knowledge and planning to write about her experiences for the *New York Globe*, a tabloid newspaper. Needless to say, Alvirah's recordings provide some crucial evidence about Leila's murder, but it is Alvirah's own voice that adds a new and interesting comic twist to Clark's fiction.

Alvirah Meehan's effusive chatter and "gutsy" sighs (31) are a crude contrast to the polite decorum conveyed in the cultured tones of the spa's wealthy clientele. Her candid observations and self-mocking confessions, however, are even more shocking to people in whom "honesty," as Elizabeth observes, "was a rare commodity" (97). As she and Elizabeth travel by limousine to the spa on the morning of their arrival, for example, Alvirah thinks nothing of volunteering the details of her rather common personal life to this perfect stranger. Nor does she make any effort to conceal her view of the people with whom she expects to mingle at the spa. Alvirah also expresses her disappointment with the famed Coastal Highway drive—"It don't look so hot to me" (32)—and her amazement at the sight of the Roman bath—"What's *that*?" (41), all in the course of their brief drive to the spa. As her first appearance in the novel clearly indicates, Alvirah Meehan injects a dose of reality into the spa's rarefied atmosphere, and indeed, Clark relies upon her voice to administer a similar tonic to her novel. Cypress Point Spa's clientele may laugh at Alvirah, but she exposes to Clark's readers the element of the ridiculous that characterizes their life, to which they are virtually oblivious. Alvirah's unintentional exposure of the Cypress Point Spa world ultimately reveals Clark's thematic intentions as well.

## CHARACTER DEVELOPMENT

In addition to these experiments with voice, Clark here forsakes the exclusively linear plot development of virtually all her previous works.

Instead of relating the sequence of events on a straight line that moves from beginning to middle to end, she relies upon the flashback to develop her central characters. *Weep No More, My Lady* begins with a prologue set in 1969, eighteen years before the immediate events of the novel. This prologue establishes the impoverished background of two loving sisters living in Lumber Creek, Kentucky. It dramatizes as well the events that caused them to escape to New York City. Then, early in the present moment of the novel in August 1987, Clark re-creates another significant occasion in the lives of the sisters, their arrival in the city that would become their new home. From these flashbacks, Clark will create the context and supply the motivation for the lives of Leila and Elizabeth.

Life in Lumber Creek, as the prologue dramatizes it, provided neither sister with much promise. There, nineteen-year-old Leila and her eight-year-old half-sister Elizabeth lived a precarious existence in a ramshackle house. The drunken brawls and passionate reconciliations of their mother and her current boyfriend added to their life's unpleasantness. One afternoon when Leila returned from her job as a waitress in a drive-in restaurant, she found her mother's boyfriend on the verge of molesting Elizabeth. That incident determined her to escape with her sister to New York and to act on her dream to become an actress. She never looked back, not even when, upon her arrival in the city, she was deceived into posing nude by a photographer who promised her a job. That false promise led her to Minna and eventually to the success of which she had dreamed. Yet Leila was never entirely able to escape her past. To the moment of her death, in fact, Leila, who had herself been abused by her mother's boyfriends (xvii), was crippled by a deep distrust of men (40) that threatened to destroy her relationship with Ted Winters. She was also plagued by a "terrible vulnerability" (115). Leila, as Sammy recalls, was a woman given to excess, a woman who had squandered two marriages. Her "outward confidence, her flamboyant public image was the facade of a deeply insecure woman" (115) who found little comfort in the trappings of her success.

Leila's one true source of satisfaction was her relationship with Elizabeth. From the beginning, their life in Lumber Creek had shaped that relationship, transforming Leila from a sister into a substitute mother to the little girl. Eleven-year-old Leila, for instance, had insisted that her baby sister be named Elizabeth and not Laverne (102). Years later, Leila, not their mother, protected Elizabeth from sexual abuse and then assumed responsibility for the child who accompanied her to New York. Later still, Leila ensured that Elizabeth attended a Swiss boarding school and had a college education, providing her sister with all the advantages that life had denied her. As Ted Winters recalls with some regret, Leila "had satisfied her maternal instincts by raising Elizabeth" (131). She would not have wanted, or indeed needed, another child.

The impoverished childhood that had bred mistrust and insecurity in Leila had created a sober and reserved Elizabeth. In Lumber Creek, the child that Leila called "Queen Solemn Face" (xiv) was old beyond her eight years. As her mother lay on the bed in a drunken sprawl with her boyfriend, Elizabeth tidied the house and then heated soup and fried hamburgers while Leila determined their next course of action (xvi). Life taught responsibility early to Elizabeth. It taught her assertiveness as well. When Leila appeared at Minna's agency to collect the fee that the bogus photographer had promised her for posing, it was Elizabeth who saved the day for her elder sister. She indignantly denounced their ill treatment not only by the photographer but also by the woman who derided their innocence (38–39). In doing so, she won Min's respect and a job for her sister.

Despite her deep love for Leila, Elizabeth had lived her life in the shadow of her sister and thus had developed her own, largely unacknowledged insecurities. When the stranger who sits beside her on the flight from Italy confuses her with another actress, for instance, Elizabeth compares herself unfavorably to her sister. She knows that nobody would have mistaken Leila for somebody else (4). Similarly, she derides her own acting ability, confessing that she feels more confident "teaching water aerobics" (108) at Cypress Point Spa than performing a part on stage or screen. So convinced is Elizabeth of her inferiority to Leila that she even fails to see that her sister's brand of beauty had been fleeting. It was, in fact, already fading at the time of her death. Her own, however, was maturing into "an elegance that goes beyond beauty" (321) and that eventually would have surpassed Leila's.

In many ways, Leila's nickname for Elizabeth, Sparrow, provides an important clue to the nature of the complex relationship between the sisters. As Ted notes of those nicknames, they always had "a double edge to them" (126). His own, for instance, Falcon, evokes a trained bird of prey, and Craig Babcock's, Bulldog, recalls the square and squat dog known for its tenacity. Leila's nickname for Elizabeth was ostensibly bestowed, like all her nicknames, as an expression of her love and regard. Because it refers to any of several small, dull singing birds, however, it suggests Elizabeth's anonymity and insignificance, and that Leila had sensed Elizabeth's own self-image.

Most of the players in Clark's drama believe that sibling rivalry, the feelings of jealousy and competition that commonly exist between the children in a family, lay behind the relationship between Leila and Elizabeth, and that Ted Winters was the immediate source of the unacknowledged competition between the sisters. All of them are aware of what Elizabeth herself fails to admit—that she had fallen in love with her sister's fiancé prior to Leila's death. All are aware as well of Leila's insecurity about her own relationship with Ted. In fact, their three-year age difference and her growing awareness of her fading beauty just as her sister's was blooming were sources of anxiety for Leila, the Baron tells Elizabeth (118). Now they believe that Elizabeth is caught in a love-hate situation with Ted and that she has accused him of Leila's murder to atone for her own betrayal of her sister's love and sacrifice.

Sibling rivalry, however, as Clark makes clear, has very little to do with Elizabeth and Leila's relationship. Rather, the mother-daughter bond accounts for its complexity. As her substitute mother, Leila had nurtured and protected her sister. She had even to some extent created her, giving Elizabeth both her Christian and her stage names and providing her with knowledge of her parentage (141–142). This deep mother-daughter bond was a source of strength for both women. Yet it also made it difficult for Elizabeth to establish her separate sense of self. Elizabeth identified with her sister. She had, in fact, become another version of her sister. But just as every daughter must sever the cord that binds her to her mother before it strangles her, Elizabeth had to discover her own strengths in order to earn Leila's respect and to achieve her own self-respect.

In addition to her skill as an actress, Elizabeth possesses other strengths and characteristics that distinguish her from her sister and on which she will draw to assert herself. She is a talented swimmer who once mounted a challenge for a place on the Olympic team. This skill eventually helps her to save herself from the killer who is stalking her. Elizabeth also possesses a reputation for honesty (91), making her dangerous to the people in Leila's circle, all of whom are quite capable of hiding their secrets and disguising their true selves. Before the curtain falls on the last act of this drama, Elizabeth, they all fear, will do whatever is necessary to discover the truth about the death of her sister. She is simply driven by her nature to expose deceit.

Elizabeth is driven as well by her deep love for Leila, and this love ultimately undermines the rumors of sibling rivalry between the sisters. As Elizabeth struggles to make sense of her own memories and the conflicting stories and surprising evidence that she uncovers, she makes an even more surprising discovery—that Leila's friends are not as distressed by her death as they appear to be. Someone, Elizabeth learns, was systematically destroying Leila's fragile hold on her world. That unknown person had been sending Leila poison-pen letters that hinted at Ted's involvement with another woman and her own fading acting talent. Moreover, everyone but Ted, Alvirah confides to Elizabeth, had joked about Leila around the dinner table (97). Shaken by these betrayals of her sister, Elizabeth vows to preserve her memory and her image. She will be the "*one faithful heart*" (109) among all these false friends and mourners. Elizabeth's decision to search for the truth, then, has nothing to do with guilt and everything to do with honor and love for her sister. She is not motivated by a childish need to surpass her sister but by a mature understanding of her feelings for the woman who had virtually given her life.

In the end, Elizabeth's decision to risk her life to expose her sister's murderer helps her to recognize her own strengths and gives her the opportunity to assert herself within the complex bond of their relationship. "In Aqua Sanitas" (100), "in water is health," is the Latin saying Elizabeth recalls during one of her late-night swims at Cypress Point Spa, and the climax of Clark's novel demonstrates its truth. The water that was meant to drown her becomes instead the element in which she is reborn her own person. In water Elizabeth does indeed find health of mind, but not at the cost of her relationship with Leila. When, in the novel's final scene, Leila speaks for the last time, she urges Elizabeth to follow her heart and embrace her own desires. She gives her approval, in other words, of Elizabeth's love for Ted Winters: "*Go ahead, Sparrow. . . . You're perfect for each other*" (360). To the refrain of Leila's song, "Weep no more, my lady," Elizabeth the Sparrow is now free to sing her own song.

Clark balances the relationship of loving sisters against that of two seemingly inseparable friends, and there she does indeed dramatize the destructiveness of jealousy and rivalry. From the time they met at college, Ted Winters and Craig Babcock have been virtually a unit. So close had they become during their years at Dartmouth that Craig, somewhat to the dismay of his friend, had perfected an impersonation of Ted's voice that made it possible to answer his telephone calls (338–339). When Ted's wife and child were killed in an automobile accident, Craig was there to assume control of Winters Enterprises when his friend was unable to function. As Ted remembers confiding in Leila at their first meeting, Craig "became my voice. He practically *was* me" (143). Years later, at Cypress Point Spa, Craig, as executive vice-president of Winters Enterprises, is still speaking for his friend. As the date of his trial draws near, however, Ted is becoming more irritated by and more uncomfortable with Craig's actions (157). He cannot even order a soft drink without having Craig contradict him (124–125).

To the larger world, Craig is the long-suffering and under-appreciated object of Ted's verbal abuse, a part he plays to perfection before Ted's lawyer, for instance (162–163), or Syd Melnick (124–125). Ted's discomfort with his friend, however, is indeed well founded, for Craig has for some time been concealing his true feelings. In fact, his long association with Ted is based more on envy and resentment than on affection and regard. As a young man, he had worked his way through college performing every sort of menial odd job (56) while his friend enjoyed the ease of his affluence. During that time, Craig had nursed to health an innate sense of inferiority born of his working-class background and a profound desire to prove his worth by attaining power like Ted's. Following college, he had achieved his position at Winters Enterprises not by presuming on his friendship with Ted, but by earning it (56). Eventually, however, Ted had begun to grow tired of his shadow. He had even realized Craig's limitations and had begun to put in motion changes that would weaken Craig's influence on the business. Determined to prevent his displacement, and angry, too, that Leila had left him for Ted, Craig found it impossible to await his inevitable destruction. Consequently, he acted to protect himself and to destroy instead those who had failed to recognize him—Ted and Leila.

These contrasting pairs of characters drive home Clark's perspective on the relationship between Elizabeth and Leila. Although Elizabeth may have lived to some extent in the shadow of her sister, she never considered Leila her rival. In fact, the only evidence that Leila perceived Elizabeth as a threat was offered by the Baron, who had his own motives for making such a claim. Rather, these loving sisters were also loving friends who may occasionally have misunderstood one another but who always wanted the best for each other. The seemingly inseparable brotherhood of Ted and Craig, in contrast, was little more than a business relationship masquerading as friendship. Because it had been forged of Craig's need, envy and resentment ultimately destroyed it (341–342). To achieve his ends, Craig simply could not allow Ted to distance himself from his shadow.

## THEMATIC ISSUES

Clark's cast of characters, as well as her plot and setting, provides ample evidence of the primary thematic focus of *Weep No More, My Lady*—the nature of true beauty. Most of the characters, for example, illustrate clearly the distinction between physical and spiritual beauty. Min and the Baron, Cheryl and Craig, have molded and shaped their bodies, nipped and tucked their flesh, cut and styled their hair. They have, in other words, done everything necessary and possible to create an attractive physical presence, to make themselves "beautiful people." Yet their beauty, as the saying proclaims, is only skin deep. As Elizabeth discovers, these members of Leila's inner circle of friends and associates had all harbored some ugly feelings for the fragile and temperamental actress, and they are now united against her (86). They are more interested in protecting themselves and achieving personal gain than in bringing to justice the murderer of the woman to whom they had professed their love and concern.

This difference between physical and spiritual beauty is emphasized by the novel's structure as well. Each section of *Weep No More, My Lady* begins with a Cypress Point Spa inspirational message and "Quote for the Day" that focus on the ideal of beauty. The quotations provide an ironic commentary on the novel's action, for as the events unfold, they undermine these noble sentiments and high ideals.

When Elizabeth arrives at Cypress Point Spa, for example, the English Romantic poet Percy Bysshe Shelley is the source of the day's quote: "Where is the love, beauty and truth we seek?" (27). The quotation, which links these abstractions, and indeed virtually makes them one, implies that they exist among the beautiful people at the spa. On the same day, however, Elizabeth learns that she has been brought to the spa on false pretenses by Min, who hopes to convince her that Ted did not murder Leila. She also discovers that those in Leila's inner circle were better enemies than friends.

On subsequent days at the spa, the quote similarly unites beauty with "joy" and "well-being" (175) and "power" (105; 287). In every case, however, the sentiments are undermined by the day's events—Dora's murder, the attempts to kill Elizabeth and Alvirah, the destruction and manufacture of evidence. Clearly, at the world of the spa, the ideal and the actual seem never to meet, perhaps because these characters have substituted physical for spiritual beauty.

The inspirational messages that accompany these quotations, all of which are penned by the Baron, certainly give evidence of just such an attitude. On Elizabeth's second day at the spa, the Baron writes that "another day at Cypress Point Spa means another set of dazzling hours dedicated to making you a more beautiful person, the kind of person people long to be with, to touch, to love" (105). The Baron's message conveys the view that beauty is a physical attribute that leads inevitably to happiness and fulfillment. Beautiful people, of course, are naturally loved and desired. Among people who subscribe to such views, however, Elizabeth will find neither love nor truth, for their physical beauty has never penetrated to the core of their being.

Clark's setting also helps to emphasize this theme. The clientele of Cypress Point Spa are the products of a regimen designed to transform them into an ideal of physical beauty that is intended to represent inner beauty as well. In other words, their beauty is artificial and manufactured, not a natural expression or reflection of their being. It is the product of collagen treatments and herbal wraps, water aerobics and massages, and even murder cannot halt this regimen. At the spa, "the business of beauty and luxury" (355) is conducted to the very end of the novel's action.

Thus Clark uses the elements of the novel to drive home her point about the nature of beauty. It is clearly more than a physical attribute. Rather, it originates "in the deep heart's core" and expresses itself in caring and concern, love and devotion, in the countless daily kindnesses that we offer to our fellow beings. It is utterly connected, in other words, to true moral character. To prove her point, Clark relies upon the actions of Dora Samuels, Elizabeth Lange, and even Ted Winters, all of whom serve as examples of true beauty in the novel. Their willingness to place themselves in jeopardy to pursue truth and justice and their insistence upon honoring the memory of the woman they loved offer persuasive evidence of the nature of true beauty. They also serve as powerful alternatives to the selfishness and deceit that lie beneath the pleasing surface of the novel's other characters. Dora, Elizabeth, and Ted are the moral center of *Weep No More, My Lady*. They are the proof of Clark's primary theme.

## A CULTURAL CRITIQUE OF *WEEP NO MORE, MY LADY*

The elements of her novel also give Clark a chance to dissect contemporary society and to offer some rather insightful cultural criticism. If we view it as a sociological document, the novel records and reflects the attitudes and behaviors of the people who inhabit the world it re-creates. Thus, the critic may examine it as an expression of culture. This critical perspective looks back to Matthew Arnold's view that literature offers a critique of life. It also bears some connection to Marxism, with its emphasis on the material foundation of a culture's ideology. It is not, however, specifically Marxist, being more appropriately linked to a tradition of American liberalism devoted not so much to doctrine or methodology as to cultural commentary.

While the field of cultural studies is not new, its recognition as a unique branch of inquiry is a relatively recent development, primarily identified with postmodernism. In other words, it has come into its own since the end of the Second World War. Generally, cultural critics apply the concepts and theories of various disciplines to the elite arts, popular culture, the media, ordinary life, and other aspects of contemporary culture and society. Cultural criticism is, according to Arthur Asa Berger, "a multidisciplinary, interdisciplinary, pandisciplinary, or metadisciplinary undertaking" (2). Consequently, it may involve literary theory, psychoanalytic theory, Marxist theory, sociological and anthropological theory. Whatever their approach or discipline, however, cultural critics seek to understand their culture and society and to explain it to those who live in it.

While this definition of cultural criticism may seem rather broad, containing so much that it cannot be contained itself, one important concept gives shape to this critical approach. Cultural criticism, as Berger notes, "is always grounded in some perspective on things that the critic . . . believes best explains things" (8). In other words, cultural critics always have some connection to, or identify themselves with, a group or discipline. Some are feminists, some Marxists, some conservatives, radicals, Freudians, anthropologists, or any combination of these groups. For the purposes of this analysis of *Weep No More, My Lady*, then, we shall approach the novel from a sociohistorical perspective that has much in common with Marxism, a theory explained in Chapter 4, but which is not specifically Marxist.

If we examine *Weep No More, My Lady* as a social and historical document, we discover that Clark has used the mystery-suspense genre to fashion a novel of manners, that is, one that focuses on the social customs, manners, conventions, and habits of a definite social class at a particular time and place, frequently in a comic or satiric vein. In other words, it uses humor or sarcasm to expose and ridicule human vices and follies. As a novel of manners, *Weep No More, My Lady* exposes a world where appearances count far more than true moral character, and thus lays it open to that critique of life that is cultural criticism.

Clark's re-creation of the world of Cypress Point Spa certainly evokes the novel of manners. This is a world of privilege and exclusivity, where patrons pay four thousand dollars a week to be pampered into health. The regimen at the spa includes collagen treatments and a gourmet diet, deep meditation and early morning walks. Here, "masseurs kneaded muscles and pounded layers of fat; pampered bodies were wrapped in herbal-scented sheets" (355). Here, too, guests luxuriate in perfectly appointed rooms, swim in Olympic-size pools, and have a large staff to cater to their every need or whim.

The world of Cypress Point Spa might not seem too extraordinary were it not for Alvirah Meehan. When she wins the lottery, Alvirah indulges a dream and heads for the spa, offering herself up to its regimen in the expectation that she will be transformed into a woman worthy of her wealth. Yet from the time of her arrival at the spa, Alvirah cannot help but expose the superficiality of this world. Clear-sightedness and plain speaking are too much a part of her nature to prevent her from calling a spade a spade.

Because she intends to share her experience of the spa with the readers of the *New York Globe*, Alvirah relates her impressions into a tape recorder each evening. Those candid comments are far more perceptive than anyone looking at her might expect. Describing the warm hose treatment, for instance, Alvirah observes that it is "another word for crowd control" (122). Alvirah also notes that the spa's landscaping and design are intended to prevent the clientele from exposing themselves to each other. The observation prompts Alvirah to remark, "I really don't care that the whole world knows I'm going to have collagen injections" (122). Others, however, would not be quite so honest about their physical appearance. Upon examination by Alvirah Meehan, the spa's every aspect falls victim to her incisive judgment.

Alvirah's complete candor about the spa makes her its worst enemy, for with every observation she unintentionally demolishes its facade. It takes no special talent, for instance, to be among the spa's privileged guests, for anyone can learn its rituals. Alvirah herself confesses to Elizabeth that she had managed to master the complex rituals of the spa's dinner table by recalling "the way Greer Garson helped herself from the fancy silver platter in *Valley of Decision*" (97). What matter at the spa are money and status, but such commodities may be entirely unrelated to substance and stature, as Alvirah's own brush with death makes clear.

In the end, Alvirah, as Sheriff Scott Alshorne observes, is "like the child in the fable *The Emperor's New Clothes* who says, 'But he has no clothes on!'" (270). In her role as truth sayer, she exposes the pretentiousness of the spa's regimen and rituals, the emptiness of the clientele's fine manners and gestures. As the comparison between Alvirah and the child of the fable makes clear, Clark intends for her character to provide an alternative perspective on the world of the spa and to bring into focus the reality that lies behind the image. Her novel needs a character such as Alvirah, to whom the manners and morals of the spa world are alien, if it is to offer the cultural critique conveyed by its setting, characters, and plot devices. It needs a character such as Alvirah to transform a tale of mystery and suspense into a novel of manners reminiscent of, for example, Agatha Christie's Miss Marple tales. And such is indeed Clark's purpose in *Weep No More, My Lady*.

Clark's sixth novel ultimately is something of a departure from her previous works, for its concerns are as much sociological as psychological. In the character development of her heroine, Elizabeth Lange, Clark continues to explore the issues of identity and self-definition that have been so much the focus of her other novels. Certainly she explores thematic issues that give depth and weight to her tale of mystery and suspense. But her setting—the exclusive world of Cypress Point Spa—and her inclusion of a character whose chief function is to make readers see the inconsistencies in it indicate Clark's willingness to use the genre for purposes other than entertainment. In *Weep No More, My Lady*, Clark examines contemporary society and exposes its tendency to value the superficial and pretentious and thereby offers us a view on ourselves and our world.

## ALVIRAH MEEHAN AND *THE LOTTERY WINNER*

A genuine original amid a host of imitations, Alvirah Meehan is one of the chief strengths of *Weep No More, My Lady*. In the early drafts of the novel, however, Clark intended her luck to run out at Cypress Point Spa. Alvirah was supposed to fall victim to a vicious killer—and her own cleverness. When her daughter Carol protested, however, Clark relented, bringing Alvirah "back from death's door" (Acknowledgments) to sleuth again in one of her 1994 best-sellers, a collection of short stories entitled *The Lottery Winner: Alvirah and Willy Stories*.

Neither time nor affluence has changed Alvirah Meehan since she nearly met her death at Cypress Point Spa. She still looks upon her world and the people who inhabit it with a mixture of droll humor and innate compassion. She still includes herself among those on whom she focuses her powers of keen observation and insightful evaluation. And she still enjoys the challenge of a good mystery. The good life now fits Alvirah like a comfortable shoe. She complains, for instance, of having to fly tourist class in the title story (180). Yet she has never forgotten her humble beginnings, and she is not afraid to return to them. In fact, the old apartment in Flushing where she and her husband Willy had lived prior to their great stroke of luck still awaits their return should fortune demand it (119).

The collection's title story, "The Lottery Winner," illustrates Clark's continuing regard for her endearing sleuth as well as her continuing preoccupation with the theme of appearance and reality that figures so prominently in *Weep No More, My Lady*. In this story, Alvirah returns to Cypress Point Spa to investigate quietly and unofficially the disappearance of the Hayward jewels. Upon her arrival, she quickly develops her list of suspects and begins to penetrate the pleasing surfaces behind which they hide their true selves. In typical Alvirah style, she notes, for instance, that Elyse, Cotter Hayward's ex-wife, "was born with a silver spoon in her mouth." She can also tell "by her voice that Nadine," the current Mrs. Hayward, "isn't a graduate of Miss Porter's" finishing school (188). As always, Alvirah is the person capable of discerning the real thing because she is herself its embodiment.

In an afterword to the collection, Clark notes that "winning the lottery changed the way Alvirah and Willy lived. But it never changed Alvirah and Willy's innate wisdom about what really matters in life." Every story in *The Lottery Winner* drives home this truth and provides examples of "what really matters"—family, friendship, honesty, good faith. Every story demonstrates that wealth does not excuse anyone from right behavior and that common human decency makes demands upon us all.

Clark illustrates these points most forcefully, perhaps, in "Plumbing for Willy." In this story, Alvirah and Willy's appearance on the Phil Donahue Show prompts the kidnapping of the former plumber. Determined to save her husband, Alvirah becomes her old self to solve the case. Dressed in tight jeans, "well-worn sneakers," and a "fleece-lined sweatshirt" (119), remnants from her pre–lottery winning life, she takes a room service job at the hotel where the kidnappers are holding Willy. Soon, she has discovered his exact location and with some assistance from an unlikely source—a group of nuns—manages to rescue him.

Forty million dollars is nothing, after all, without the man she has always loved.

In the end, the wry humor of the stories in *The Lottery Winner* is a pleasing change of tone from Clark's more characteristic somberness, and Alvirah Meehan certainly accounts for the difference. She still views her world and herself with the eyes of a realist who cannot be deceived by appearances. Nor is it in her nature to be anything other than herself. The humorous tone of these stories, however, does nothing to detract from Clark's seriousness of purpose. In their themes and concerns, they are, in fact, characteristic. Yet it is clear that whenever Alvirah Meehan appears, the characteristic takes on a new life. Perhaps that is why Clark allowed her to live to sleuth again.

# 9

## *While My Pretty One Sleeps*
### (1989)

In *While My Pretty One Sleeps*, her seventh tale of mystery and suspense, Mary Higgins Clark journeys into the world of high fashion to explore familiar territory—the dark underside of an industry devoted to beauty. Once again, she exposes the superficial glitter that camouflages the greed and ambition, the deceit and betrayal that are so much a part of the flawed human beings who compete in this world. In doing so, she extends the primary theme of *Weep No More, My Lady*, the novel immediately preceding this one. *While My Pretty One Sleeps*, however, does more than merely travel down old paths. It also forges some new trails, the most important of which lead to an examination of the complex relationship between parent and child and the terrible burden of guilt.

When Neeve Kearny, the owner of an exclusive Madison Avenue boutique, begins investigating the mysterious disappearance of Ethel Lambston, one of her best clients, she hasn't a clue about where her enquiries will lead her. In fact, she is uncertain about whether she is even justified in making them. Only her own intuition and knowledge of her quarrelsome client's habits give evidence that Ethel's disappearance is anything more than a scheduled holiday or business trip. Yet Neeve is convinced that something is wrong. The problem is that nobody but Neeve seems to care that the best-selling author of hard-hitting exposés is missing. In fact, Ethel's ex-husband Seamus, her feckless nephew Douglas Brown, and especially the top fashion designers Gordon Steuber and Anthony della Salva, whose secrets Ethel is about to reveal, all have their reasons to be glad that she is gone. Even Myles Kearny, Neeve's father, the retired New York City police commissioner, cannot work up any concern for the sardonic writer who had once pursued him. Yet when Ethel Lambston's body is discovered with her throat slashed in a suburban state park, Neeve's investigations suddenly take on new urgency, for they unintentionally place the young woman in mortal danger. Before the novel ends, however, Neeve will have discovered the truth about Ethel's disappearance, faced the unknown menace in her own life, and solved the mystery of her own mother's murder seventeen years before.

## NARRATIVE STRATEGIES TO CREATE MYSTERY AND SUSPENSE

Suspense is the result of a writer's ability to evoke fear and uncertainty about the fate of the protagonist. Its creation depends upon the author's handling of the novel's elements. In typical fashion, then, Mary Higgins Clark relies upon two of her standard techniques, an endangered heroine and the constraints of time, to create and build suspense in *While My Pretty One Sleeps*.

The life of Clark's resourceful heroine is imperiled. Someone has placed a contract on Neeve Kearny, and throughout the novel, a killer with a deadline stalks her. Neeve, of course, is entirely unaware of the threat against her. Even if she knew of it, she would never suspect that Denny Adler, the young man who delivers her lunch from the local deli, has been hired to kill her. Only chance prevents him from successfully completing his mission on any number of occasions. As he comes under increasing pressure to finish the job, however, it seems only a matter of time until he murders his unsuspecting victim.

To complicate her typical narrative strategy, Clark includes a character whose knowledge of the contract could save Neeve, but who is incapable of telling what he knows. Tony Vitale, an undercover policeman who had infiltrated the world of organized crime, could be Neeve's savior. He is present on the day that Nicky Sepetti, the crime boss whom Myles Kearny wrongly holds responsible for his wife's murder, is released from jail and makes his triumphant return to his Mafia family. Informed about the contract, Sepetti is horrified. He knows that given his history with the Kearny family he will be held responsible for the murder even though he is innocent of it. Vitale is privy to this interchange and could warn Kearny of the threat to Neeve's life. Sepetti, however, knows instinctively that this new family member is not what he appears to be and orders the informer's execution. Throughout the novel, then, Vitale lies in a hospital bed clinging to life and trying desperately to regain consciousness to tell what he knows before it is too late. His presence provides an image of the powerlessness that frustrates Clark's readers, who, like Vitale, know the truth but cannot divulge it.

In addition to relying upon these common strategies for creating and building suspense, Clark gives a new twist to the narrative structure of *While My Pretty One Sleeps*. For most of the novel, nobody but Neeve believes that a crime has been committed. Readers, of course, know that Ethel Lambston is dead because the first chapter details the crime and the disposal of the body. But until her body is discovered two-thirds of the way through the action, nobody has any logical reason to believe that Ethel has been the victim of foul play. In fact, Ethel's habits and personality make it seem far more likely that she has simply disappeared to conduct some research.

Delaying the discovery of the crime gives Clark the opportunity to unfold her cast of possible suspects in such a way that they all appear guilty. Although he has no reason to believe that his aunt has left town (unless, of course, he is the criminal), Douglas Brown has taken up residence in Ethel's apartment and is even sleeping in her bed. Seamus Lambston, Ethel's ex-husband, and his wife Ruth make several trips to Ethel's apartment, and Ruth even tears up the alimony check that Seamus had mistakenly delivered to the woman who had been his tormentor for more than twenty years. All of these characters had motive and opportunity to commit the crime. Consequently, their lack of concern about Ethel's disappearance casts a shadow of doubt on their actions, even when there appears to be no reason for doubt.

## CHARACTER DEVELOPMENT

Clark's narrative strategy also emphasizes key elements of her characterizations, particularly her depiction of Neeve Kearny. In the face of everyone's doubt or unconcern, Neeve trusts her intuition that something has happened to Ethel. Thus, neither the gentle teasing of her father nor the insolence of Ethel's nephew can deter her from responding to it. She possesses the strength of character to stand firm on her beliefs and to overcome any obstacle, and her self-possession will see her through her ordeal.

Neeve's response to Ethel's disappearance also reveals her genuine concern and compassion for others. Ethel has certainly done little to endear herself to others. She uses her pen as a weapon, subjecting others to her sarcasm and ridicule, and even Neeve admits that the sixty-one-year-old writer can be exasperating. Yet she also glimpses and responds to the fragile humanity that lies beneath Ethel's prickliness. When, for example, Ethel "wistfully" confesses that Seamus had denied her the children that she had always wanted, Neeve understands the hurt that has hardened her (30). Similarly, when she learns that nobody ever remembers Ethel's birthday, Neeve perceives her essential loneliness (122). When nobody else can find room in his or her heart to care for Ethel, Neeve finds herself missing her sharp-witted client and regretting her own failures of friendship toward her. These responses testify to her essential humanity.

Neeve's concern for others is wedded to high moral principles that she will not compromise. At one point, she learns that the renowned designer Gordon Steuber is running an illegal sweatshop and exploiting children as laborers. The knowledge prompts her to cancel the order she had placed for his designs and to mail him "a copy of the Elizabeth Barrett Browning poem which had helped change the child-labor laws in England" (29). Although Anthony della Salva warns her against making a powerful enemy in Steuber, Neeve will risk both her livelihood and her life to stand firm on the right and to champion the good.

In this respect, Neeve is clearly her father's daughter, for Myles Kearny has given his life to the pursuit of crime and has paid dearly for his devotion. As police commissioner, Myles had earned a reputation for scrupulous honesty and an unswerving commitment to duty. Seventeen years before, Nicky Sepetti, the Mafia crime boss, had threatened to kill Myles' wife and child if he went to jail. The police commissioner, however, had not hesitated to expose Sepetti and secure his conviction. The murder of Renata Kearny two weeks after Sepetti's conviction was cause for Myles' deep regret, not because he had pursued a criminal, but because he had failed to take the criminal's threats seriously. Seventeen years later, Myles has not altered his perspective on either Sepetti or his own behavior, but he has learned to be more cautious. He is now doubly careful to protect Neeve from harm but is still willing to put himself at risk for principle. Although he has just recovered from a heart attack, he is considering an offer to head a federal drug enforcement program.

In addition to their high moral principles, father and daughter share an essentially romantic nature, for both believe in true love. Myles had found his true love in Renata Rosetti, the young Italian girl who had nursed him to health after he was wounded in the Second World War. Thirteen years after that ten-year-old girl had saved his life, Myles returned to Italy to discover the woman he seemed destined to love. Within three weeks, they married. As she faces her ordeal, Neeve, too, will find her true love in Jack Campbell, the president and publisher of Givvons and Marks and a man with whom she shares almost uncanny similarities and tastes. On one occasion they find themselves wearing identical sweaters and slacks, a coincidence that prompts Myles to call them "Flossie and Freddie Bobbsey" (243). Such similarities are clearly intended to convey Clark's belief, as she confessed in an interview, "that some people are meant for each other" (*Loves Music* interview n.p.). Reflecting this belief, her central characters are unabashedly romantic. Neeve and Jack fall in love in a matter of days, as do Myles and Kitty Conway, the attractive widow who discovers Ethel's body.

To emphasize the romantic nature shared by father and daughter, Clark evokes their Celtic heritage, particularly the degree to which its superstitions and myths inform their lives. Throughout the novel, both Myles and Neeve have premonitions of death that they credit to their Irish heritage. Myles cannot "shake off the nagging worry that had been growing in him for weeks" (32). This feeling he associates with his grandmother's "sixth sense" and his cousin's death in Ireland. Similarly, Neeve is "vaguely distressed" by a "throbbing pain somewhere in her psyche." It causes her to "[grumble] to herself, Before long, I'll really be one of those superstitious Irish, always getting a 'feeling' about trouble around the corner" (59). She also senses her own death on several occasions (230, 253). These premonitions enhance the novel's suspense by creating an atmosphere of eerie otherworldliness. More important is their revelation of the emotional and spiritual legacy that connects all the generations of Kearnys.

The Celtic origins of Neeve's name also underscore the romantic longings and beliefs of Clark's characters. As Neeve explains to Jack, her name is an Americanized version of Niamh (185–186), the Celtic goddess associated with the "Land of the Young" or eternal life (Squire 225). According to Celtic myth, Niamh of the Golden Hair, as she was known, was the daughter of the son of the Sea and a creature of more than human beauty. Mounted on a fairy horse, she captured the love of Ossian. He rode with her to the land of the gods and dwelt there with her for three hundred years before he remembered his homeland and his people. Filled with longing to see them again, Ossian begged leave of

Niamh, who permitted him to return to Erin but warned him against touching his feet to earth. When Ossian fell to the ground from Niamh's fairy steed, he was immediately transformed into a withered old man, and the goddess abandoned him to his fate, the death that awaits all mortals (Squire 223–226).

As this most famous of the myths associated with the goddess suggests, Niamh/Neeve possesses the power of the enchantress, and she promises a poetic immortality with her love charms. Yet woe to the lover who forsakes her, for Niamh has no pity. This lesson is not lost on Jack. Teasing his own Neeve, he says, "I'm beginning to think you *are* the legendary Neeve who leaves her admirers behind as she rides away" (188). Clearly, a belief in true love has been passed down through the generations to both the Kearnys. The myths live anew, in fact, in each generation, embodied in those who believe.

For all their similarities, father and daughter are sharply divided—Myles has virtually no regard for Neeve's fashion sense and thus for her career. He finds fashion frivolous. In the larger scheme of things it simply cannot compare with catching criminals and enforcing the law. Throughout the novel, Myles and Neeve engage in good-natured disagreements about this issue. Neeve, however, is absolutely correct in her assessment of its real significance. "Myles," she observes, "was the world's leading chauvinist" (113). This aspect of his character will be particularly important to Clark's development of theme.

## THEMATIC ISSUES

Despite their friendly bickering, neither Myles nor Neeve allows their essential difference of opinion to interfere with their loving relationship. This characteristic serves to dramatize one of Clark's stated purposes in *While My Pretty One Sleeps*—to explore the nature of family relationships. "I created a strong father-daughter relationship," observes Clark, "because I am tired of books about parents and children at each other's throats" (*Loves Music* interview n.p.). This relationship, then, serves as the thematic focus of the novel.

On one level, the interaction between Myles and Neeve illustrates Clark's point. At the age of twenty-seven, Neeve still lives comfortably, but quite independently, in the apartment she has always shared with her father. Following his heart attack, she has been more than willing to forego some of her own activities to nurse her father back to health.

Myles is protective but not overbearing, and each of them respects the other's freedom and wants only the best for the other.

Despite Clark's stated intention, the parent-child relationship in *While My Pretty One Sleeps* is more problematic than it appears to be. Neeve has clearly achieved her goals without the support of her father, the most important man in her life. Although Neeve was quite happy at home, Myles, as she tells Jack, "fought tooth and nail to send me away to college." Consequently, she attended a small private college and even studied abroad. Similarly, although Neeve "always knew what [she] wanted to do" (187), as she confesses to Jack, her father did not approve of her career choice. She had turned to her father's childhood friend, the man she calls Uncle Sal, Anthony della Salva, for the financial support to establish her boutique, Neeve's Place. Her father, characteristically, discouraged her from accepting the loan. So while Neeve and Myles may not always be at each other's throats, neither do they share an ideal parent-child relationship. Myles is so convinced of his own perspective that he accepts but cannot admire his daughter's accomplishments.

Her father's grudging acceptance of her career choice is clearly a source of disappointment for Neeve. Myles' statement that Renata wasted her life "selling clothes to bored women" also reflects negatively on Neeve. Feeling the sting of her father's judgment, Neeve thinks to herself, "I've been written up in *Vogue, Town and Country, The New York Times* and God knows where else, . . . but that doesn't cut any ice with him" (113). Then she nurses her own wounds, seeking to recover the self-esteem her father has undermined. Although Neeve will excuse Myles' judgment by calling it chauvinistic (113), the fact that she must do so is evidence of her deep need to hold his love.

To some extent, Uncle Sal functions as substitute father to Neeve. At the very least, this supportive male is the ideal model to counteract her own father's barely concealed contempt for her career. A renowned designer known for his Pacific Reef Look, Uncle Sal shares Neeve's passion for fashion. It was he who took her to fashion shows, loaned her the money to fulfill her dream, and advised her to develop a reputation for exclusivity. Uncle Sal is not without his faults, but as a source of professional support for Neeve, he clearly bests his childhood friend, and Neeve takes comfort in his counsel.

Clark's exploration of the parent-child relationship is also complicated by the presence of the parent who is not there. Although Renata was murdered seventeen years before, Neeve's response to Ethel's disappearance suggests that the young woman has never entirely faced her own loss. Her mother's cookbooks, for instance, with their "notations in Renata's bold, curlicued hand," are a source of pain for Neeve. In addition to the annotations, the margins of the pages are filled with Renata's sketches of her daughter. "Charming, beautifully drawn miniatures" (112), they evoke "a sense of profound loss" (113) in Neeve. For years she has simply avoided them in an effort to escape her pain.

Now Ethel's murder causes Neeve to remember the other murder that so changed her life. Walking with Jack in Central Park, Neeve tries to avoid the place where Renata died. When she cannot, she has a vivid flashback of the ten-year-old girl who waited at school for the mother who never came to pick her up (196) and experiences again her terrible sense of loss. Ethel's murder opens an old wound, perhaps because it has never completely healed, and also because the quarrelsome writer had been like Renata in an important way. Both women, in their acceptance and encouragement of Neeve's interests and talents, had validated the young woman's sense of self. To lose Ethel is to lose again someone who has nurtured her development.

Thus, Clark's exploration of the relationship between parent and child is far more complex than she may have intended it to be. Despite their deep love, Neeve and Myles disappoint each other, and that fact is especially troubling to the child. Although she may shrug off her hurt, Neeve looks to others for the support and acceptance her father fails to give her. From this perspective, then, the relationship between Neeve and Myles is flawed rather than ideal, and it dramatizes the power of the parent to give shape and meaning to the child's life and self, the central theme of *While My Pretty One Sleeps*.

Two other themes emerge, one of which Clark previously explored in more detail in *Weep No More, My Lady*. In setting her novel amid New York City's world of high fashion, Clark once again exposes its dark underside. One designer, Gordon Steuber, runs an illegal sweatshop, uses child labor, and traffics in heroin. Another, Anthony della Salva, routinely takes credit for the work of those he employs and even commits murder to steal another's work. The world of high fashion that Clark reveals is competitive and cruel. Greed and ambition abound here, and the beautiful clothing is merely camouflage, concealing corruption.

A third theme, the burden of guilt, is also important in *While My Pretty One Sleeps*. Guilt may account at least in part for Anthony della Salva's generous support of Neeve. Having stolen Renata's designs and taken her life, Uncle Sal may be attempting to purchase forgiveness by giving her daughter the resources she needs to establish her career. Yet his subsequent actions indicate that guilt has never burdened him much. Rather, the boy who allowed a friend to take the blame when he broke Myles' arm years before (125) had grown into a man who justified anything to advance his career and to protect himself from exposure.

For Myles Kearny, however, guilt is a destructive weight that prevents him from living his life fully. Seventeen years after Renata's murder, Myles continues to blame himself for failing to protect her. Adding to the unbearable burden of his guilt is the fact that as its commissioner he had at his command the full resources of the police department, and yet he could not solve the crime. For seventeen years, Myles' "one unfulfilled need" (23) has been to find the murderer and secure justice for his wife.

Nicky Sepetti's release from prison and the subsequent threat to Neeve's life give Myles the opportunity to make amends for his previous lack of vigilance. In doing so, he is also able to release himself from the death-in-life that has been his self-imposed punishment. Following the heart attack that kills Sepetti, Myles visits the site of Renata's murder and experiences "for the first time in this place . . . a tentative sense of healing" (127). In response, he assures the spirit of Renata that their child is safe. Then, having recalled some lines from a poem by Alfred, Lord Tennyson, that speak directly to the pain of death-in-life, he vows to put the past behind him and to move forward in life. When he is there at the end to save Neeve from almost certain death, Myles is truly released from his burden of guilt. As the world bursts forth with new life in springtime New York at the novel's end, Myles has fully recovered from his own heart attack and is planning a new life with Kitty Conway in Washington, D.C. With these details Clark signals the rebirth of a man who has finally forgiven himself for his own failures.

## A FEMINIST READING OF *WHILE MY PRETTY ONE SLEEPS*

The issue of Myles' guilt as well as his relationship with his daughter raises some interesting questions if viewed from a feminist perspective. A feminist critic would focus on Myles' chauvinism as the reason he has failed both his wife and his daughter; it has prevented him from recognizing, appreciating, and encouraging their talents. To the extent that he denies their needs and efforts to fulfill their own desires, Myles is neither the ideal husband nor the ideal father.

Neeve remembers clearly her father's belittling of Renata's interests, for she had herself felt the sting of his disapproval. On one occasion when Neeve is skimming the delightful sketches with which Renata had annotated her cookbooks, for example, Myles observes that her mother should have studied art rather than wasting her talent. Rising to Renata's defense, Neeve asserts, "Mother liked what she did," to which Myles retorts, "Selling clothes to bored women" (113). In that instant Neeve acknowledges her father's chauvinism and its effect on their lives: "If Renata had pursued art," Neeve reflects, "if she'd developed into a mediocre painter of watercolors, he would have considered it a ladylike hobby. He simply couldn't understand that helping women select becoming clothing could make a big difference for those women in their social and business lives" (113). Clearly, both Renata and Neeve labored despite Myles rather than with him, for his expectations of them were far below those they had for themselves.

While Myles' chauvinism has hurt his daughter, it has not prevented her from pursuing her dream. For Renata, however, Myles' attitude had far more deadly consequences. When Renata took the designs that would eventually become his "Pacific Reef Look" to Anthony della Salva, this family friend killed her for them. He also killed Ethel Lambston and intended to kill Neeve to avoid exposure. Renata's talents were far superior to his own, Uncle Sal tells Neeve as he prepares to murder her, but she had "[wasted] all that knowledge on a clod like your father who can't tell a housedress from a coronation robe" (305–306). And so Renata had died, the victim of greed and ambition and the aggressively male world of cutthroat competition that della Salva and Gordon Steuber represent. Myles is responsible, in a sense, for Renata's death, not because he failed to protect her but because he failed to recognize and appreciate her gifts and thereby made her vulnerable to exploitation and abuse.

The fate of Renata and Ethel clearly testifies to the destructiveness of paternalistic chauvinism as well as cutthroat competition. Expecting women to channel their talents into "a ladylike hobby" (113) denies them the opportunity to develop their human potential. Similarly, when women speak the truth and pursue a goal as brashly as their male counterparts, they are criticized for being assertive and deemed unworthy of concern because they have stepped beyond the bounds of decency for their sex. Renata and Ethel are both victims of stereotypical beliefs about appropriate roles and behavior for women. These beliefs, frequently disguised as the kindness and concern of a father for his daughter, may be well-meaning, but they are nonetheless restrictive. As if to emphasize the point, the vital clues to the mystery of Ethel's and Renata's murders hinge on fashion, the female interest upon which Myles heaps such disdain: Renata is killed for her fashion designs; by choosing the wrong blouse, Ethel's murderer exposes himself.

A feminist interpretation of *While My Pretty One Sleeps* would also take a critical view of the very concept of fashion that figures so importantly in Neeve's life. When she reflects that "becoming clothing could make a big difference for . . . women in their social and business lives" (113), Neeve confirms another truth about gender limitations and expectations. To succeed in the world, women must dress the part. Their ability to advance, in other words, depends as much on their physical appearance as on their intellectual accomplishments. Given this perspective, Myles' view of fashion as something too frivolous to warrant consideration may be seen as progressive. To his mind, what people wear should have little bearing on our view of them. The skills, talents, and habits of mind that each person brings to life are what matter.

Such a view of gender equality, however, is far removed from Neeve's rather blind acceptance of the message of fashion. She seems never to have questioned the stereotypical notions about women that are revealed in her own career choice. Moreover, her perception that clothing is an expression of personal style (210) suggests that she would discount this feminist critique of fashion, and so, I believe, would Clark. Her characterization of Neeve is too positive to undermine her career, and the role that fashion plays in the mystery equally validates it. Feminists may turn a critical eye on the assumptions that uphold the world of Clark's heroine, but Clark would not.

By the end of *While My Pretty One Sleeps*, both the living and the dead are at peace. The murderer of Renata and Ethel has been brought to justice, and his apprehension releases them all from their private pain. For Myles especially, release from his burden of guilt makes it possible for him to let Renata rest, and when she is no longer merely sleeping, he can move forward in his life. Myles' release also frees Neeve from his desperate protectiveness and opens the possibilities for a different sort of father-daughter relationship. The restoration of order and the renewal of love with which the novel ends clearly signify Clark's belief in true love, her hope for happy endings. In *While My Pretty One Sleeps*, both are indeed real.

# 10

## Loves Music, Loves to Dance
### (1991)

In 1975, Judith Rossner's cautionary tale *Looking for Mr. Goodbar* exposed the dark underside of one of that decade's social phenomena, the singles bar. Sixteen years later, Mary Higgins Clark focused her attention on the latest dating trend—the personal ads  to issue her own warning note in *Loves Music, Loves to Dance*, her eighth novel of mystery and suspense. As an examination of the singles scene, *Loves Music, Loves to Dance* is a chilling tale of sexual harassment and murder. It explores the consequences of "the pace of modern living," which, according to Clark, provides "less and less opportunity to meet others through traditional channels—family, friends, community" (*Loves Music* interview n.p.) The novel moves beyond its contemporary subject, however, in its examination of the relationship between its central characters and in so doing offers an affecting meditation on the nature of true friendship. It extends as well the exploration of the complex relationship between parent and child that Clark began in her preceding best-seller, *While My Pretty One Sleeps*.

When Darcy Scott persuades her best friend Erin Kelley to conduct research for a documentary on the people who place and answer personal ads and their experiences, neither is prepared for the consequences. Following graduation from Mount Holyoke, the former college roommates move to New York City to establish their careers. Erin, a jewelry designer, and Darcy, an interior decorator, are just beginning to taste success. Then, Nona Roberts, a television producer at Hudson Cable Network and a fellow dance classmate, asks her friends to date some men through the personal ads as research for her latest documentary. Darcy convinces a reluctant Erin that doing so will be a lark. Several weeks later, however, Erin goes missing, and when her body is recovered on a Manhattan pier, Darcy is driven by guilt to find the person who murdered her. Convinced that Erin's death is connected to her personal ad dates, Darcy determines to meet the men Erin dated. One of them, she feels sure, left her friend lying on a pier wearing her own shoe on one foot and a high-heeled dancing slipper on the other. Before long, Darcy's investigations lead her to several possible suspects and into mortal danger, for the serial killer who entices his victims through the personal ads has targeted Darcy as his next victim.

## NARRATIVE STRATEGIES TO CREATE MYSTERY AND SUSPENSE

A personal ad serial killer provides Clark with the perfect plot device around which to build both mystery and suspense. The element of the unknown in the personal ads makes it possible to cast suspicion on a diverse group of characters. Any one of the minor characters, including a shoe buyer for a large department store who had responded to Erin's ad, could be the killer. So, too, could a university maintenance man who begins to make harassing telephone calls to Darcy and even attempts to accost her in the lobby of her apartment building following their brief first date. From the beginning, however, probability focuses on three primary suspects, all of whom are rather unlikely.

Jay Stratton, a jeweler who places personal ads to meet potential clients, may be a thief and a con man, but murder seems far outside his mode of operations. Doug Fox, an investment banker and self-styled "prince of the personals" (16), is interested only in escaping a boring marriage and the responsibility of four children in suburban Scarsdale—and in evading detection. Least likely of the primary suspects is Michael Nash, a psychiatrist who is conducting his own research on personal ad dating for a book on the subject. Charming and cultured, he, too, had dated Erin. Now he becomes the sympathetic confidant of Darcy, who is strongly attracted to him.

Into the mix of potential suspects, Clark adds Gus Boxer, the "sixty-year-old Casanova in dirty flannel" (30) who works as superintendent

of Erin's apartment building. Ten years before, he had been superintendent of another building where a young woman was murdered, so now
he becomes one of the police's prime suspects. Any one of these men
had the opportunity to murder Erin. Any one of them, in spite of appearances, could be Charley, the chilling psychopath who has murdered
not only Erin but also Nan Sheridan and seven other young women in
a killing spree that began fifteen years before. Any one of them could be
Charley, who plans now to make an unsuspecting Darcy his final victim.
So full, so diverse, and so carefully constructed is her list of suspects
that Clark keeps the reader guessing the killer's identity until the novel's
terrifying climax, one of the key requirements of a good mystery.

Because Clark generally emphasizes suspense over mystery, readers
usually know the identity of the criminal long before the protagonist
discovers it. This knowledge, in fact, generates the uncertainty and anxiety characteristic of suspense. In *Loves Music, Loves to Dance*, however,
Clark creates the situation of the classic "whodunit." Withholding the
identity of the criminal is one of its primary conventions. It provides
readers with the opportunity to match wits with the detective or the
protagonist and to solve the crime from the clues. By keeping readers in
the dark, Clark thus devises a mystery from which to elicit her suspense.

The novel's climax, when it comes, is classic Mary Higgins Clark. In
fact, she has been constructing it from the novel's beginning. In her efforts to trap Erin's killer, Darcy, as the reader knows, is playing right
into his hands, for the first chapter of the novel reveals the mind of the
murderer and his evil intent. Readers learn that Charley still suffers the
pain of his mother's rejection (3) and that he blames Nan Sheridan for
what he has become. "If only Nan had liked him" (1), he laments to
himself. They learn as well that Charley intends to mark the anniversary
of that first murder with a final murder, and that anniversary is less than
a month away.

What gives a twist to Clark's typical strategies for creating and building suspense here is that Darcy Scott is not an unsuspecting victim. From
the moment she determines to lure Erin's killer into exposing himself,
she has understood and even welcomed the danger she faces. While the
killer's deceptive nature will ultimately undermine her vigilance, it will
not defeat her. Because Darcy distrusts every one of her and Erin's personal ad dates, she functions from a position of power, unlike so many
of Clark's heroines. Thus, the reader never really doubts her ability to
accomplish her mission.

## CHARACTER DEVELOPMENT

As the heroine of *Loves Music, Loves to Dance*, Darcy Scott is believable, engaging, and sympathetic. The only child of two famous stars of stage and screen had a privileged upbringing. Yet as Vince D'Ambrosio, the FBI agent investigating the case, notes, Darcy is the real thing: "Nothing Hollywood about that girl" (129). If anything, the heritage of Darcy's background has been a lack of self-confidence resulting from a childhood incident. As a six-year-old, she had once "overheard a director comment, 'How ever did two such stunning people manage to produce that mousy-looking child?'" (7). Darcy never forgot that childhood hurt, and through the years, her own mother's attention to her daughter's appearance (6, 131) magnified the slight. As she tells Michael Nash, "I always felt like a changeling [at her parents' Bel-Air mansion], as though the princess daughter of the royal couple must be living in a cottage and I was an imposter in her place" (176). Only now, with the success of her business, Darcy's Corner, Budget Interior Design, is Clark's materially privileged but emotionally impoverished heroine beginning to come into her own.

Darcy's transformation is due at least in part to her friendship with Erin Kelley. As college roommates, they develop a relationship that becomes the chief source of support for both, drawn together, no doubt, by their many similarities. Both share an artistic temperament, and both are virtual orphans. Erin's father lies comatose in a nursing home suffering the effects of multiple sclerosis. Darcy's parents have seldom been a presence in her life. Both women also love music, love to dance. Although chance brings them together, Darcy and Erin are soon "closer than sisters" (10).

Despite the ties that bind them, these fast friends differ in one significant aspect. Darcy is far more adventurous than Erin, who frequently suffers the consequences of her roommate's daring. During their senior year of college, for instance, Erin fell and broke her leg because she succumbed to Darcy's urging and made one last run down an icy ski slope at Stowe. Now Erin is missing because she reluctantly agreed to participate in Darcy's personal ad dating scheme. Needless to say, Darcy is consumed by guilt on both occasions, and that guilt drives her to jeopardize her life to trap Erin's killer.

## THEMATIC ISSUES

The relationship between Darcy and Erin is central to the development of Clark's major theme in *Loves Music, Loves to Dance*, for despite its contemporary subject, the novel is a moving exploration of the nature of true friendship. Clark signals this theme's importance in the novel's opening quotation by the Greek philosopher Aristotle: "What is a friend? A single soul dwelling in two bodies." The quotation speaks to the intense spiritual bond that unites two people who have shared confidences and experiences, who have exposed their most private selves to each other in a relationship of absolute trust. Those who develop such a bond exemplify the friends of which Aristotle speaks. In *Loves Music, Loves to Dance*, Darcy and Erin are without doubt Clark's true friends.

From their chance meeting to their violent separation, Darcy and Erin nurtured and sustained one another's emotional and professional development. Each understood the other's insecurities and helped her to overcome them. After they became roommates, for instance, Erin realized that Darcy was far less self-confident than she appeared to be. Designer suits and Italian shoes may have given her a look of sophistication, but Darcy felt like an imposter in such clothing. Moreover, her mother's insistence that she wear it confirmed her own sense that she was a deep disappointment to the "golden couple" (97). Yet as Darcy muses to Vince D'Ambrosio after she identifies Erin's body, "Erin urged me to be more daring about clothes" (95–96), a comment that reveals the degree to which her friend had helped her to learn to wear her clothing with style by supporting her fragile sense of self. Darcy's friendship had worked similar magic on Erin.

The only child of a mother who had abandoned her because she was unwilling to accept the responsibilities of an infant daughter and an invalid husband, Erin was raised by a father who was losing his battle with multiple sclerosis. Bright and talented, she had attended Mount Holyoke on scholarship. The circumstances of her life thus combined to make Erin in her own way as insecure as her privileged roommate. She once confessed to Darcy that "she felt so out of it when I walked in the room with my folks that first day at college" (95). Although Darcy admired Erin's own "smashing" ensemble, she ultimately had to teach her "to trust her own instincts," her own "impeccable taste" (95, 96).

Their friendship cemented during college, Darcy and Erin continued to rely upon each other as they attempted to establish their careers in

New York. No longer roommates, they shared confidences over the telephone virtually every day, met frequently for dinner, and together attended ballroom dancing lessons at their health club. So deep is their mutual trust that Darcy knows the location of the combination to Erin's safe; Erin has also made her friend executor of her will. For her part, Darcy has promised to assume responsibility for Erin's father should anything happen to her friend.

When Erin is murdered, then, Darcy's determination to trap the killer has as much to do with friendship as with guilt. Robbed of her other self, Darcy simply cannot stand idly by in hopes that the police will capture an elusive criminal. Instead, she directs her deep sense of loss and outrage toward avenging her friend's death, and in so doing honoring her life.

Clark embodies her major theme and the truth of Aristotle's statement in the friendship of Darcy and Erin. United by choice, not by blood, these two young women forged a friendship as strong as any sibling relationship. In fact, to some extent their friendship was a substitute for familial relationships that were missing or ineffectual in their lives. Yet as Vince D'Ambrosio tells Darcy, "In my business I've observed that having one good friend can beat having a passel of relatives" (65). Clark would agree with such an assessment.

The contemporary nature of her subject matter also gives Clark the opportunity to issue a dire warning about personal ad dating. In an interview, Clark noted that she chose her subject because "people in all walks of life are turning to personal ads to find romance or companionship," but that such ads are "risky." Because those who respond to personal ads "are taking on faith what a stranger tells [them]," Clark believes that "meeting strangers on an anonymous basis is dangerous, especially for women." They can easily "fall prey to sexual harassment, rape, even murder" (*Loves Music* interview n.p.).

In the course of her research for *Loves Music, Loves to Dance*, Clark consulted with one of the FBI's top criminologists, an expert in serial murder and violent crime. She learned from him that at least one serial killer had "enticed his victims through personal ads." She also learned of other women who had become homicide victims after responding to personal ads. Clark incorporates this information into her novel, which lends it a chilling sense of authenticity.

Clark's depiction of the serial killer, for instance, matches exactly the profile given by D'Ambrosio, an FBI agent linked to the Bureau's Violent Criminal Apprehension Program (VICAP): "well-educated; sophisticated; late twenties to early forties; physically attractive" (56). Although they may never have been arrested for a violent crime, they may have a juvenile history of voyeurism or fetishism. They may also make photography their hobby.

Such a description could have been written from the biography of Michael Nash, the serial killer "Charley." So charming and cultured is the psychiatrist that nobody would suspect him of having another, darker self. That other self, who loves movie musicals and imagines himself a Fred Astaire, wooing and winning his lady love on the dance floor (46), has suffered the pain of his mother's rejection (3) as well as a similar slight from Nan Sheridan, his first victim. Now he searches the personal ads to find the perfect partner, a woman pliant enough to match her steps to his. Unable to find her, he is driven by frustration and rage to murder those who reject him. He films their dance of death to relive it again and again and replaces one of the victim's shoes with his signature dancing slipper. The serial killer that resides within Michael Nash is the horrifying embodiment of every woman's worst nightmare. And as the novel makes clear, women who search for love and companionship in the personal ads risk the nightmare.

Through the plot devices of Nona's documentary and Darcy's search for the killer, Clark offers sufficient information about personal ad dating to deter even the most foolhardy. Yet her cautionary tale is not without hope for love and romance. Erin's murder unites four strangers with a common purpose, and as they learn about each other, two couples are formed, without the help of personal ads.

When Nona Roberts meets Vince D'Ambrosio, both are still hurting from recent divorces. Nona, a television producer, has lost her husband to a younger woman. Vince's job at the FBI has been the undoing of his marriage. Drawn together by her documentary and Erin's murder, Nona and Vince find themselves attracted to each other, perhaps because they share not only interests but also vulnerabilities. By the novel's end, they have begun to establish a basis of mutual trust, support, and companionship upon which to build a relationship of love.

Darcy Scott and Chris Sheridan also have in common the serial killer, for both are his living victims. Fifteen years before he murdered Darcy's best friend, the killer had danced with his first victim, Chris's twin sister Nan. Thus, both know the pain of the survivor, the ache of loss. Their tentative but promising relationship, however, overcomes their losses, and flourishes on respect, admiration, and mutual interests.

Thus, the relationships between Nona and Vince and Darcy and Chris are the perfect foil to those that exist potentially in the personal columns. Common interests and purpose rather than a specific mission to find the perfect companion draw these characters together. Moreover, because they are under no pressure to fulfill the usually exaggerated claims of a personal ad, these characters can simply reveal themselves as they are. Finally, the very conventionality of these relationships testifies to Clark's belief in the traditional ways of finding a companion, despite the pace of modern living and the anonymity of contemporary society. In Nona and Vince and Darcy and Chris, Clark offers a tribute to old-fashioned love and romance.

## A PSYCHOLOGICAL READING OF *LOVES MUSIC, LOVES TO DANCE*

Clark's portrait of a serial killer and her exploration of friendship are particularly revealing when viewed from the perspective of the psychological critic. Such critics apply the methods of the psychoanalyst to the study of literature. They examine the mind of the author, the minds of the author's characters, and our own minds as we read the text and seek in psychoanalysis the secrets of the literary work. This perspective is particularly appropriate to *Loves Music, Loves to Dance*, for Clark's characterizations depend upon her use of the double to give depth to their meaning.

As inseparable friends, Darcy and Erin are indeed Aristotle's "single soul dwelling in two bodies." Yet they may also represent the opposing sides of that same soul. In Freudian terms, Darcy is the id, the part of the unconscious that seeks immediate gratification of her impulses, even those that may be self-destructive. Erin is the superego, the part of the unconscious that creates an ideal self and that functions as well as a conscience, registering approval or disapproval of one's actions. These friends are, in other words, Freud's pleasure principle and reality principle embodied.

In her frontal attack on life's experiences, Darcy does indeed seem to court disaster to satisfy an inner drive to surmount any obstacle. Icy slopes and falling darkness will not prevent her from skiing, nor will admonitions of danger prevent her from personal ad dating. Even when Erin's death offers convincing evidence of that danger, even when the police warn her against her plan, Darcy simply will not abandon her efforts to trap the killer. Whatever its shape, "no" is a challenge to Darcy; she refuses to accept limitations and prohibitions.

As Darcy's cautious, responsible other half, Erin is the socially acceptable ideal self that controls—or at least tries to control—her irrational and self-destructive impulses. She must be persuaded to tackle that icy ski slope and to risk the personal ads. In the struggle between having a good time and being a good girl, however, the appeal of the former is too strong to resist. Erin does what she knows she should not do and inevitably suffers for her actions.

As the ultimate "no," Erin's murder initially stands as a challenge to Darcy's better judgment. Indeed, it is almost as if her conscience has been murdered, and so she plunges headlong into her attack. But the guilt that motivates Darcy to place her life in danger is ultimately a reassertion of conscience. This reassertion leads Darcy to a profound acceptance of limitation and responsibility, proof of which Clark offers in her heroine's new understanding of her own parents.

On one of her first personal ad dates with the psychiatrist Michael Nash, Darcy finds herself confiding and indeed confronting some long-repressed feelings of resentment and abandonment that she had harbored against her parents for years. Darcy realizes that she has been "subconsciously blaming [her] mother and father all these years" (232) for the insult she suffered as a child. Later, to save herself from the killer, Darcy, like Scheherazade (286), will trap him in narrative, weaving a net of stories about her troubled relationship with her parents that captures the psychiatrist's attention and delays his evil act. Darcy's stories, however, all reveal the terrible truth from which she has been hiding.

Telling Nash of the time she lost her mother's hand in a crowd of fans, Darcy confesses, "I was so frightened. I couldn't see them. I knew that moment that I hated . . . The crowds. Being torn from them. . . . If they weren't so famous . . . " (285). She also recalls the sense of abandonment she experienced when she was hospitalized at the age of six (288–289). In response to his observation that she may have been "trying to shut them out" (289) as punishment, Darcy then wonders, "Had she? Always resisting the clothes her mother bought for her, the gifts they showered on her, scorning their lifestyle, something they'd worked all their lives to achieve. Even her job. Was that one-upmanship to prove something?" (289). Darcy believes that she is pretending to enact the role of patient to Nash's psychiatrist when she tells him these personal stories. Yet the truth is that she has, however unintentionally, become his patient. As she reflects to herself, "I don't want to talk about this, . . . but I must" (285).

Darcy's ordeal forces her to confront the demons in her psychic past and to take responsibility for her childish alienation from her parents. By accepting her own limitations, her own responsibility, Darcy can also accept her parents'. No longer is she the child who demanded absolute attention to her needs—and who frequently saw slights where none was intended. Thus, she can honestly speak her love to her parents at the end of the novel (304). In understanding herself for the first time, Darcy has come to understand them.

Clark offers a parallel use of the double in her killer, the man who calls himself Charley but whom the world knows as Michael Nash. In his aggressive sexuality, Charley clearly represents the id. He needs and demands immediate gratification of his urges, and failing to achieve it, he vents his feelings of rejection by killing the objects of his thwarted desires. The psychiatrist Michael Nash is the superego. He understands and can even to some extent control his dark urges. As the two selves struggle for mastery of the ego, however, Nash is simply unable to repress Charley. Angered by reports that Erin's is a copycat murder, Charley thinks, "It is I, Charley, alone who has the power of life and death over these women. I, Charley, broke through the prison of the other soul and now dominate him at will" (91). In the struggle for control, Nash, the superego, ultimately disappears.

The source of the Charley/Michael conflict is his parents. When his father murdered his mother, one-year-old Charley was adopted by his aunt and uncle and became Michael Nash. Years later, at puberty, Michael was made to feel embarrassed about his sexuality by his adoptive mother. In fact, he associated her subsequent rejection of him with her discovery of his sexual fantasies (3) and her conviction that "bad blood shows" (292). Eventually, Michael killed his adoptive parents in retaliation for their rejection of him (293). His Charley self simply cannot cope with hurt and rage, the inevitable consequences of what he views as mistreatment.

Clark's use of the double to convey the psychology of *Loves Music, Loves to Dance*'s central characters allows her to explore further the complex relationship between parent and child. Her previous novel, *While My Pretty One Sleeps*, revealed a parent's unintentional failures. This novel suggests that the child must come to see and to accept the parent as a person to achieve psychological growth and maturity. Into adulthood both Darcy and Michael have childishly continued to blame their parents for childhood hurts. In doing so, they have hurt themselves. Michael, for instance, never accepts responsibility for what he has become, continuing to blame others—his victims, his parents—for his actions. Consequently, he eventually loses his ability to control Charley and slips into madness. Darcy, in contrast, eventually recognizes her own responsibility for the distance between herself and her parents and accepts their shortcomings. When she achieves this understanding, Darcy has clearly come under the influence of her better self, her adult self, and is ready to move ahead in life.

*Loves Music, Loves to Dance* is, then, far more than a cautionary tale about personal ad dating. Rather, in its presentation of the intricacies of the self, it explores the nature of human relationships to reveal their complexities as well. Yet in spite of its serious thematic issues, Clark never forgets that she is writing a novel of mystery and suspense, an entertainment intended to drive readers relentlessly to its satisfying conclusion. Here she certainly does not disappoint. As Joyce Cohen asserts in her review of the novel, "This Cinderella story turned sour reaffirms that Mary Higgins Clark deserves her reputation for creating splendid suspenseful fiction" (16).

# 11

# *All Around the Town*
## (1992)

Mary Higgins Clark's ninth best-selling novel was inspired by a request for an autograph. An art therapist specializing in the treatment of multiple personality disorder once asked Clark to sign a book for one of her patients. When she asked for the patient's name, the therapist, as Clark recalls, could not remember which of her patient's many selves was a fan of Clark's novels. The response aroused Clark's interest, and soon she was exploring the subject in a story that became *All Around the Town*. That innocent request for an autograph eventually led Clark—and her readers—into an examination of the very mysteries of personality, for they lie at the heart of this somber tale of innocence betrayed.

When Laurie Kenyon, a twenty-one-year-old college student, is accused of murdering her English professor, Allan Grant, she has no memory of the crime. Abducted at the age of four, Laurie was subjected to two years of abuse and incarceration by Bic Hawkins, an unsavory drifter, and his wife, Opal. To protect herself from the horrors of that life, she developed multiple personalities, of which Laurie, the host personality, is utterly unaware. Grant's murder, however, triggers an exploration of the mysteries of self. When her fingerprints are discovered everywhere at the crime scene—on the door, on the curtains, on the knife used to stab the handsome professor—Laurie is arrested. Immediately, attorney Sarah Kenyon resigns her position as assistant prosecutor to defend her younger sister. Her strategy is to prove that Laurie's childhood trauma was the direct cause of Grant's murder, so she calls in Dr. Justin Donnelly, a specialist in the treatment of multiple personalities. Soon he discovers that "Leona," one of Laurie's other selves, had been writing crazed love letters to Grant and that she had even been secretly entering his home. This evidence may persuade a jury to exonerate Laurie of the crime. As Donnelly helps Laurie to retrieve and to confront her repressed memories, however, he unintentionally places her in mortal danger. Bic Hawkins has never forgotten Laurie. Moreover, he has now transformed himself into another personality, a celebrated television evangelist with everything to lose should Laurie break through her tortured past. Hawkins has no intention of allowing that to happen.

## NARRATIVE STRATEGIES TO CREATE MYSTERY AND SUSPENSE: TIME AND PLOT

### Time

In *All Around the Town*, Clark departs from her typical narrative strategy, a limited time frame, to meet the demands of her subject matter. A serious psychological problem, multiple personality disorder does not develop spontaneously, nor can it be diagnosed and treated overnight. Rather, as Clark's plot makes clear, a person with the disorder may function normally for years until some shocking event shatters the host's personality, thereby allowing the other selves expression (57). For the sake of realism, then, Clark begins her novel seventeen years prior to the murder and extends the main action over a period of nearly a year. Part One details Laurie's abduction and two-year captivity. Part Two begins fifteen years later with the crucial event—the accidental death of her parents—that shatters Laurie's unified self and prompts her other personalities to surface. It ends with the murder of Allan Grant. Part Three focuses on Sarah's defense of her sister and Dr. Donnelly's efforts to heal an innocent victim.

### Plot

Yet despite this necessary departure from her signature strategy, Clark creates a novel that is no less suspenseful than her previous works by relying primarily upon the subject matter itself. As Laurie undergoes treatment for her disorder, readers find themselves fascinated by the exposure of her many personalities. They are eager to learn which of them killed Allan Grant, for one surely must have done so. They want to know, too, whether Laurie's condition will eventually spare her from punishment, so they rush to the novel's end to learn the solution to the mystery.

The mystery readers rush to solve, therefore, is not who murdered Allan Grant but rather the mystery of Laurie Kenyon, the mystery of personality. Indeed, so fascinated are they by the novel's unfolding of personality that they may fail to notice that, unlikely as it may seem, Grant's murder is little more than a red herring, a plot device intended to blaze a false trail, to create suspicion where none in fact should exist. Granted, Laurie is clearly implicated in the crime, and she even convinces herself that she killed her professor and pleads guilty to murder. Nevertheless, neither she nor any of her various personalities is actually involved in the crime. Thus, when the police finally crack the case, the killer's identity is obvious, and the solution to the mystery is rather unsatisfying because Allan Grant has never really mattered as a character. Moreover, although the murder is solved, the mystery of personality remains unresolved.

*All Around the Town* is a novel with so many twists, so many false resolutions of plot, that it comes as no surprise when Clark has one more thrill planned for her readers. To achieve it, she relies upon the press of time and the endangered heroine, the hallmarks of her suspense. Just when it seems that Laurie will finally find the happiness she deserves, Clark brings her face to face with her worst nightmare. Bic Hawkins has lurked in the shadows of her past and on the edge of her life for too long. Until she confronts him, the curtain cannot fall, as it must, on her drama of self. Thus, when their horrifying confrontation does occur, it leads ultimately and inevitably to the satisfying resolution of the novel's true mystery.

## CHARACTER DEVELOPMENT

The mysteries of personality that drive the plot of *All Around the Town* are necessary to Clark's development of character in the novel and particularly to her portrayal of Laurie Kenyon. The four-year-old child kidnapped from the safety of her suburban home had been carefree and friendly and perhaps a bit spoiled, but understandably so. Her parents had considered her their "miracle" (6). After fifteen years of childless marriage, John and Marie Kenyon had long since given up hope of becoming parents when a first daughter, Sarah, was born to them. Eight years later and well into their forties, the Kenyons believed the birth of Laurie more than answered their prayers, and the whole family showered the child with love and attention.

During the two years of captivity detailed in Part One of the novel, Laurie suffered every sort of physical, emotional, and sexual abuse. She was locked in the basement, chained to a pipe, when her abductors, Bic and Opal Hawkins, left the house. She was beaten and yelled at when she cried and even made to watch the slaughter of her pet chicken. Forced by her abductors to call herself Lee, the carefree and innocent Laurie was systematically erased. In her place came other personalities into which she could escape from the horrors of her life.

Released by her abductors because they feared exposure, Laurie returned to the embrace of her family an anxious and distrustful six-year-old. The morning after her return, however, she awakened with absolutely no memory of her ordeal. She had simply repressed two years of her life. So unwilling were her parents to face the truth about the abuse she had suffered that they accepted their daughter's denial of the past. Laurie Kenyon was born again that morning. The cost of her transformation would only be known years later, when the deaths of her parents shattered Laurie's fragile sense of self.

From the time of her abduction, Laurie had assumed responsibility for what had happened to her. She believed herself guilty because she had disobeyed her parents and run down to the street in front of her home to wave to a passing funeral procession. When her parents are killed in an automobile accident seventeen years later, Laurie is again tortured by guilt. This time her failure to have her vehicle inspected placed the responsibility on her aging parents. The inspection complete, they died in a traffic accident while delivering her car to her at college. Guilt over their death elicits her previous guilt and causes her to lose her fragile hold on herself. When she whispers to herself at the funeral, "Mommy, Daddy, I'm sorry. I won't go out front alone again" (23), Laurie has already begun to disappear. What follows is not so much character development as the eventual integration of a self.

Even before Allan Grant's murder, Sarah had begun to fear for her sister's sanity and insisted that she see a psychiatrist. Laurie was once again having a nightmare from childhood, what she called her "knife dream" (33). Frequently when Sarah telephoned her sister at college, she was unable to reach her, although Laurie claimed that she had been studying in her room all evening. Moreover, Grant had told Sarah of his conviction that Laurie was sending him crazed love letters. So when he is found murdered and all the physical evidence implicates Laurie, Sarah knows what she must do to save her.

Under the treatment of Justin Donnelly, Laurie begins to confront her past by exposing the various personalities residing within her. Four-year-old Debbie, for example, is "the little girl lost" (323). She is also the most fragile of Laurie's others. Kate is strong, realistic, and resourceful. She is, as Dr. Donnelly tells Laurie, "self-preservation" (323). Although sexual abuse has left her fearful of men, Laurie's own sexuality has merely been repressed, not erased. Leona, the self who had been infatuated with Allan Grant, is "the woman" in her, the "sex kitten" (323), as Laurie eventually admits.

Most troubling and troubled of all her personalities, however, is the nine-year-old alter ego whose name Laurie refuses to speak. This child holds the secrets to a pain too great for any one self to bear, but during her ordeal, he had borne it. When Laurie was subjected to sexual abuse, this self, a brave little boy, had protected her, "always [sending] her away when Bic hurt her" (310), and he continues to protect Laurie into the present by refusing to give the names of her abductors. At the murder scene he also collects a bracelet that he believes is Laurie's but is really the killer's. This little boy is Lee, the self she became to please her abductors, and he holds the missing pieces to the puzzle of her past. Only when Laurie finally names him is she able to fit the pieces together for good.

The clue to the mystery of Laurie's several selves lies in the novel's title, taken from the old song "The Sidewalks of New York." When she was abducted, Laurie was carrying a music box that played the tune. Its lyrics, which were first used by Bic to mock her (5), eventually gave a way to cope with her ordeal. As the song's lyric promises, "boys and girls together" suffered Laurie's fate—she did not face it alone. In fact, as she tells Dr. Donnelly, "That's why the others came to be with me. We were boys and girls together" (310). That lyric prompted four-year-old Laurie to create in her mind a supporting cast of characters with whom to share her pain, her fear, her loneliness. They had helped her to survive.

Laurie's struggle to unify her several personalities into one whole is the primary focus of characterization in Clark's novel. Equally touching, however, is Sarah Kenyon's own quiet struggle for selfhood. The twenty-nine-year-old assistant prosecutor gives every appearance of being ca-

pable and self-confident. Yet almost from the moment Dr. Donnelly
meets Sarah, he recognizes that this poised and intelligent young woman
is suffering her own private pain. As he treats Laurie, he will also lead
Sarah to some necessary truths of her own, truths that will help to free
her from the past and give her her own life. Just as it always has, however, her struggle toward selfhood takes place in the background of Laurie's tragedy.

From the time of Laurie's birth, Sarah had suffered in silence the painful recognition that her younger sister was special. Sarah's birth, as her
mother had explained to her, was a "gift," but Laurie's was "a miracle."
Later, when the second-grader one day asked her teacher, "Which was
better, a gift or a miracle?," Sister Catherine confirmed what Sarah had
instinctively known: "A miracle is the greatest gift a human being can
receive." The answer prompted immediate tears in a little girl who
"looked like neither of her parents" (6).

Despite her painful knowledge, Sarah "loved her parents fiercely," so
to keep their love and approval, she bargained with God, promising to
be a perfect child if He would not take her aging parents from her before
she reached adulthood. One part of that promise, however, to "help take
care of Laurie" (6), would haunt her forever. As much as she loved her
sister and watched over her, Sarah could not prevent her abduction. In
fact, on the day Laurie was kidnapped, Sarah was at a friend's birthday
party. She had let down her guard and her sister was gone.

Laurie's abduction shattered the lives of John and Marie Kenyon and
left Sarah with a terrible burden of guilt. She sought refuge in her school-
work and in sports, but she simply could not help wondering "if God
was punishing her for the times she'd resented all the attention paid to
Laurie." Nor could she stop hating herself for her failure to protect her
sister. Hoping to redeem herself, Sarah promised once again that if God
gave them another miracle, if He returned Laurie to them, she would
"always, *always* take care of her" (9). Sarah had spent her life taking care
of Laurie from the moment of her sister's return.

On the day of Laurie's homecoming, for instance, Sarah assumed the
role of an adult protector. She cooked her sister's favorite meal and dec-
orated her room with all her favorite toys, understanding instinctively
that Laurie might feel estranged from her past. Later in the evening,
when she witnessed Laurie's fear, she cautioned her parents against pres-
suring their daughter to resume her place in the family circle before she
was ready to do so. Years later, when Laurie's life is again collapsing

around her, Sarah continues to play her well-rehearsed part. She even sacrifices her job to defend her sister from the menace in her life.

Clearly, Sarah had grown old too soon. Laurie's birth and then her abduction had saddled her with a burden of guilt and taught her painful lessons about the limits of love. The adolescent who had silently disappeared from Laurie's bedroom on the night of her homecoming had recognized in her parents' complete absorption in their youngest daughter her own insignificance (20). That wounded teen had grown into a woman whose self-sacrifice indicates a lack of self-esteem. Sarah may appear strong and poised, but as Dr. Donnelly notices immediately, she cannot conceal "the pain in her eyes hinting at . . . grief and anxiety" (65). Readers know that her pain has as much to do with her own life as it does with Laurie's.

Sarah's self-sacrifice, however, ultimately earns her a reward. Laurie's successful struggle to achieve psychic wholeness frees Sarah from her guilt. Her recognition that Laurie no longer needs her relieves her of a kind of crushing parental responsibility. From that point, she is able to acknowledge her love for Dr. Donnelly and to plan for a future of her own. She is able, in other words, to truly live her life.

## THEMATIC ISSUES

The development of her two principal characters provides Clark with the perfect opportunity to explore one of the primary themes of *All Around the Town*—the terrible burden of guilt. Both Laurie and Sarah are crippled psychologically because they have assumed responsibility for events over which they had no real control, and neither can forgive herself for failing. Laurie blames herself for both her abduction and her parents' deaths. As she tells Dr. Carpenter, one of her psychiatrists, "Two things went wrong in my life. In both cases I'm to blame. I admit it" (38). Similarly, Sarah believes it was her fault that her younger sister was kidnapped. If only she hadn't resented her sister's special status, if only she hadn't abandoned Laurie to attend a birthday party. "If onlys" fuel the guilt of these innocent victims and very nearly destroy them.

Clark makes clear that neither Laurie nor Sarah was responsible for the evil force that invaded their lives and robbed them of their innocence. Both Dr. Carpenter and Dr. Donnelly advise Laurie to view her situation rationally. A four-year-old child could not be responsible for the actions of adults (38, 303). To emphasize her point, Clark even links to it the criminal case that Sarah is prosecuting at the beginning of the novel, involving a young woman who had been murdered by a stalker. When Sarah wins a conviction, she fears that the criminal will be sentenced leniently because he intends to blame the victim for his actions (112). That excuse, so far as Sarah is concerned, is unjustifiable. Victims simply cannot be blamed for their victimization.

The burden of guilt, however, cannot be eased by right thinking alone. To free the conscience we must forgive ourselves, Clark makes clear. No other forgiveness will do. This is the lesson Dr. Donnelly imparts to Laurie when they watch as a little girl, totally absorbed in bouncing a ball, wanders too close to a busy street and then strikes up a conversation with two strangers. The child has, of course, been cautioned to do neither. Dr. Donnelly reminds Laurie that she was once that little girl. Then he urges her to "forgive yourself as readily as you would forgive that child if something she couldn't help had happened to her today" (303). By the end of the novel, both Laurie and Sarah have taken to heart Dr. Donnelly's lesson and have begun to heal themselves by forgiving themselves.

*All Around the Town* also examines the power of the unexplored past. Although sexual abuse caused Laurie's multiple personality disorder, her parents' failure to face the truth about their daughter's victimization worsened her condition. When Laurie is reunited with them, John and Marie Kenyon refuse to admit what they had surely been told by the doctors who examined their daughter. In fact, Marie Kenyon created a pleasant fiction to explain Laurie's abduction. Someone, she insisted, who had loved and wanted a child certainly had cared for her. As Sarah tells Dr. Carpenter, "Mother needed to believe that" (32). Yet her mother's need to believe a lie conflicted with her daughter's reality, so Laurie never received the help that would have made emotional and psychological healing possible. As a result, she had buried her past and hidden her boys and girls, destroying herself in the process.

Like other Clark heroines, from Nancy Harmon to Katie DeMaio to Pat Traymore, Laurie must finally confront her past to survive, and this she does in the novel's terrifying climax. When Laurie faces Bic Hawkins, her worst nightmare becomes reality. The knife in her mind is there now before her, and Bic urges her to turn it upon herself, to pay the price of her guilt. Paralyzed by her conflicting selves, Laurie is again ready to be a victim. When Sarah enters the room and Bic threatens her, too, Laurie acts to save her sister and also saves herself. By the novel's end, having faced her past, Laurie has truly emerged whole from her nightmare. In a "firm voice" that suggests strength of self, she can honestly say, "It's really over" (340).


## A PSYCHOLOGICAL READING OF *ALL AROUND THE TOWN*

By its very subject matter, *All Around the Town* lends itself to psychological analysis, most particularly Jungian analysis. In her development of character, Clark suggests that each of us creates a persona or a social self that reflects the role that we play in life. This persona, according to Carl Jung, the man who identified it, masks the individual's true inner self and the parts that animate it. Jung called those parts the Anima, or the feminine side of the male Self; the Animus, or the masculine side of the female Self; and the Shadow, a demonic image of evil that represents a side of the Self that we reject. According to Jung, each of us is in search of psychic wholeness, that state of being during which these four principal archetypes are unified. That search leads typically to another archetype, the Night-Sea-Journey, a voyage from life through death to rebirth. For Jung, this pattern repeats itself endlessly in the basic motifs of the Quest, the Shadow, and the Night-Sea-Journey as the individual seeks his or her goal of Self.

From a Jungian perspective, Laurie's abductor, Bic Hawkins, is dramatized almost exclusively as a persona. He creates false selves which are intended to conceal the shadow self that is his reality. The forty-five-year-old television evangelist now looks every bit the preacher. He has come a long way from the day he and his wife, two "hippie types" (13), kidnapped a little girl and robbed her of her innocence. Then they were Bic and Opal, two guitar-playing drifters on the make. They had worked first at cheap bars in New Jersey but were soon "gospel singing at revivals and then preaching in upstate New York" (28). They were about to start a religious program on a small radio station in Bethlehem, Pennsylvania, and begin their climb to the top when Bic could not control his obsession with Laurie's blond loveliness. Two years later, on their way to a "fifteen-thousand-watt station in Ohio" (11), Bic reluctantly released Laurie, but only because he feared exposure.

Almost immediately, Bic and Opal began their transformation into respectability as Bobby and Carla Hawkins. Bic shaved off his beard and cut his hair short. Carla dyed her hair ash blond and twisted it into a neat bun. In their "sensible clothes" purchased "at JC Penney," they achieved "the middle-American look" (29). Bic also learned to set his face in the proper expressions of deference, respect, and piety, and "taught himself to stand very straight so that he always seemed to stand above people, even taller men." He even "practiced widening his eyes when he thundered a sermon" (27) until that look became habit. Fifteen years later, on the verge of success, Bic has his persona firmly in place.

As the language of these passages indicates, Bobby and Carla Hawkins are well-rehearsed players in their life's drama. They have created the self-images they intend to project to the world. So calculated, in fact, are their external selves that they share a "private joke"—"It's a little too Betty Crocker"—"when they wanted to impress the congregations who came to hear him preach" (28). Yet these personas simply cannot disguise completely the shadow selves that truly define Clark's villains.

When Sarah first meets the Hawkinses, for instance, she responds instinctively and correctly to Carla's tasteful suit and stylish hairdo. Thinking "mutton dressed as lamb" (198), she recognizes that Carla is not what she appears to be and is masquerading as someone younger. Similarly, although the charismatic Bobby is better able to conceal his shadow self, his hairy arms are the visible symbol of his predatory nature. Thus, when they emerge again as Bic and Opal in the novel's climactic scene, readers are not surprised by their physical appearance.

Opal's expensive and tasteful designer sheaths have been replaced by "a short black skirt and a T-shirt that [hugs] her breasts." Her stylish hairdo has now fallen into its true state, "long, stringy dark hair, tousled and uncombed, [hanging] limp on her shoulders." Similarly, Bic has abandoned his stylish suits for "shiny black chinos unbuttoned at the waist, [a] soiled T-shirt exposing his curly-haired arms." His bare feet and the "dull gold earring" (332) dangling from his ear provide clear evidence of his true self.

As they are developed, Bic and Opal Hawkins are examples of the Jungian Shadow self. Demonic images of evil, they represent a side of the Self that we normally reject, concealing it behind a socially acceptable persona. As Clark's villains, however, Bic and Opal make no attempt to confront or to reject their Shadow selves. Their physical transformation, in fact, has no bearing on their spiritual being, a fact that Clark signifies by the irony in Bic's chosen career. As a television evangelist, Bic preaches holiness and salvation, but his words are as superficial as his appearance. From his lips, "Amazing Grace" is a perversion, for he is irretrievably lost, never to be found, never to be free.

Laurie, in contrast, embarks, however reluctantly, on the quest that will bring her to psychic wholeness. Her various personalities clearly represent the multiple selves Jung describes. In her case, however, the persona breaks down. The "Laurie" that contains and controls the various selves can no longer perform her function. When this disintegration occurs, she must, with Dr. Donnelly's help, confront those other selves in order to achieve an integrated self.

In psychoanalysis and therapy, Laurie takes that Night-Sea-Journey that brings her face to face with her "boys and girls." She must acknowledge even her most frightening other, Leona, the sexual self capable of jealousy and perhaps revenge. She must also face her nightmare, which she does in the novel's climax as her various selves fight for supremacy. Debbie cries, and Kate derides. Lee protects, and Leona urges a self-inflicted punishment. But the power of Sarah's love finds Laurie and silences the voices, pulling her back to herself (337). When she finally emerges from the night, and in her case, the nightmare, she is reborn a new and stronger Laurie. She is found and free.

The traditional hymn "Amazing Grace" rather than the popular tune to which the title alludes is ultimately the key to *All Around the Town*. Its lyrics speak of salvation, of a spiritual rebirth that makes possible a new and better existence. In *All Around the Town*, Clark offers a secular version of this archetypal story. Laurie makes a psychological journey both liberating and saving, one that transforms a little girl lost into a young woman found. In that journey, Clark demonstrates that the deepest mysteries of all reside within the self.

# 12

# *I'll Be Seeing You*
## (1993)

In Mary Higgins Clark's tenth best-seller, *I'll Be Seeing You*, nothing is what it appears to be. A dead man sends flowers from his watery grave. Identical twins are born three years apart to different women. A reporter investigates the murder of a woman who could be her, so closely do they resemble each other. Little wonder, then, that a novel that shares its setting and subject matter with an earlier work, *The Cradle Will Fall* (1980), is far more than a medical thriller. While reproduction technology is the topical subject matter of both novels, *I'll Be Seeing You*, a touching tale of duplicity and betrayal, has far more in common with *While My Pretty One Sleeps* and *Loves Music, Loves to Dance*. Like them, it focuses on the complex bond between parent and child to explore its powerful legacy. The result is a tale tempered by painful but liberating truths.

When television news reporter Meghan Collins finds herself staring unexpectedly into the face of her mirror image, an unidentified stabbing victim rushed to the emergency room of a New York City hospital, horror soon gives way to apprehension. It appears that she, rather than the victim, may have been, and continues to be, the target of a murderer. Determined to discover the victim's identity and to unlock the even more puzzling mystery of their obvious connection, Meghan enlists the help of Dr. Jeremy MacIntyre, a genetic research scientist. Her search becomes linked as well to a story she is producing about the Manning Clinic. This assisted reproduction facility boasts a remarkably high success rate in helping childless women conceive through in-vitro fertilization. Doctors at the Manning Clinic have recently ventured into the cloning of embryos, and now a woman will soon give birth to the identical twin of her three-year-old son. Eager at first to assist Meghan, Dr. George Manning withdraws his cooperation when Dr. Helene Petrovic, the embryologist in charge of the laboratory, abruptly quits. Several days later, when Dr. Petrovic is found shot to death, Meghan is unexpectedly linked to a scandal that erupts at the clinic. The executive search firm headed by her father, Edwin Collins, had placed Dr. Petrovic at the clinic. For nearly a year, Collins has been missing and presumed drowned in the Tappan Zee Bridge disaster, but now suspicion arises about his disappearance. First, Catherine Collins, Meghan's mother, receives flowers and telephone calls from the husband who is supposed to be dead. Then Edwin Collins' gun and auto are linked to Petrovic's murder. Soon the police are focusing all their efforts on finding a "dead" man, and so, too, is Meghan—but each for different reasons.

## NARRATIVE STRATEGIES TO CREATE MYSTERY AND SUSPENSE: PLOT

At least in part a medical thriller, *I'll Be Seeing You*, like *The Cradle Will Fall*, depends upon realism to create suspense. Readers must believe that the events in the novel could indeed occur if they are to experience the fear and anxiety that are the hallmarks of suspense. To achieve her effect, Clark provides her readers with straightforward explanations of the reproduction technologies that have made possible test-tube babies and genetic engineering. Although in-vitro fertilization once was a concept suitable only for science fiction, the birth of Louise Brown in England in 1978 made it a reality and ushered in an era of other seemingly futuristic developments. Today, surrogate mothering and prenatal genetic manipulation have altered our understanding of the mysteries of conception and birth. For most of us, however, cloning, or the development of a second embryo after it has split from one originally developed through in-vitro fertilization, still seems "a little like something out of *Brave New World*," as Meghan herself admits (39). Yet even here Clark makes such realities plausible, if a bit unnerving.

By focusing on the impending birth of a clone, the blue-eyed, golden-haired genetic match to Dina Anderson's three-year-old son Jonathan, Clark attaches a human face to scientific experimentation. She then reinforces its reality by making it the subject of Meghan's investigative report. As Meghan conducts her research, she learns about cryopreservation, or the freezing of embryos, and other breakthroughs in assisted reproduction. She learns as well that divided birth, or cloning, has already succeeded in England (46); all of this information is shared with Clark's readers, thereby making the strange familiar.

Yet the body of a woman whose face is the mirror image of Meghan's does nothing to dispel a profound distrust of genetic engineering, and from such distrust Clark builds much of her suspense. If the dead woman was Meghan's clone—and there seems no other possible explanation—then who is responsible for the deception that must surely have taken place? How is it possible that two exact replicas exist, seemingly independent of each other? These questions and others confound Meghan and are the source of a profound psychological unease. That anxiety is increased by the very real probability that a young woman is dead because she bears an uncanny resemblance to Clark's heroine, a feeling shared by readers, for whom the situation makes real their deepest fears about reproduction technologies.

Clark enhances the unease evoked by her medical subject with a subplot surrounding the birth of Dina Anderson's clone. The subplot includes the scandal at the Manning Clinic, the murder of Dr. Helene Petrovic, and the impending birth of a child to her niece, Stephanie. Dina Anderson gives birth to a healthy boy with a shock of bright red hair, obviously not the clone of her golden-haired Jonathan. Immediately, all of the difficult legal and moral issues surrounding the new reproduction technologies surface. A profound love of children may have motivated Dr. Petrovic to falsify her credentials (30), and the terrible mishap that resulted in the scrambling of cryopreserved embryos may have been beyond her control. Nevertheless, Dr. Petrovic has engaged in a conspiracy made possible by the new reproduction technologies. She has helped to sell embryos and has even recruited her niece to bear a child intended for someone else. This illegal and unethical traffic, with its accompanying exploitation of young women willing to rent their uteri, evokes the dreadful reality of the brave new world. When Dr. Henry Williams, the director of an assisted reproduction center, admits to Meghan, "Sometimes I wonder if we don't go too far" (114), he gives voice to the doubts that many harbor about such experimentation.

*I'll Be Seeing You* lacks a fully developed "mad doctor," one of the standard characters in the medical thriller. Nevertheless, Clark is clearly working within its tradition when she demonstrates the ease with which good intentions—in this case, the effort to assist childless women—can be corrupted by greed. When those who are entrusted with power over life prove themselves unworthy of such trust, deception and death follow. From just such a plot does Clark develop her novel's suspense. She increases it by linking that plot to Meghan, thereby using one of the conventions typically found in her works, the endangered heroine.


## THEMATIC ISSUES

In *I'll Be Seeing You*, character development is subsumed in thematic issues, particularly Clark's exploration of the parent-child relationship. Consequently, the development of individual characters is minimal. Clark's endangered heroine, Meghan Collins, is in many ways virtually indistinguishable from many of her other heroines. A young woman in her late twenties, Meghan is bright and articulate and driven to achieve her professional goals. A lawyer by training, she abandoned a Park Avenue law firm six months after joining it to pursue the broadcasting career that excited her interest and suited her talents. After three years of reporting for WPCD radio, Meghan is about to realize her dream of attaining a television anchor position when what should be a routine news story plunges her into mystery and danger. Throughout the novel, however, Meghan remains essentially the same self-possessed young woman. Her ordeal simply gives her the opportunity to draw upon her strength of character and natural resourcefulness to set her world aright.

While Meghan herself is sketched in broad strokes, her relationship with her parents, and particularly with her father, is etched in fine detail. Indeed, this is the case with virtually every other parent-child relationship in the novel. Such emphasis indicates Clark's thematic focus. To examine it fully, she provides three additional examples and thereby delineates the legacy of this complex bond.

The relationship between Dr. Jeremy "Mac" MacIntyre and his son Kyle, for example, is nearly ideal. As the divorced custodial father of a seven-year-old, Mac understands that his son misses his mother, who has seen him only three times since she left them shortly after his birth. As a result, Mac takes "special care and special pride in being a good, attentive father" (18). He and Kyle share weekly rituals, such as Friday evening dinners at Catherine Collins' Drumdoe Inn, which have firmly cemented their relationship. They also provide Kyle with the stability and the reassuring certainty of his father's continuing presence in his life. Mac does all he can to protect his son from some ugly adult truths, but he is never dishonest with Kyle. Rather, he treats him with the proper mixture of love, respect, concern, support, and trust, helping him to develop into a responsible and compassionate human being.

The MacIntyres' mutually satisfying parent-child relationship stands in stark contrast to the destructive bond that links Bernie Heffernan to his elderly mother. Bernie, a thirty-five-year-old parking attendant at Meghan's workplace, has been in and out of juvenile detention homes, psychiatric facilities, and prison since he was a teenager. His problems are directly related to his troubled family life. Abandoned by her husband shortly after the birth of their son, Mrs. Heffernan grew bitter and reclusive. Bernie, who still lives with his mother in the shabby house in Queens where he was born, has "to endure her incessant reminders of all the inequities life had inflicted on her during her seventy-three years and how much he owed her" (11). The burden of his debt has caused Bernie to hate his mother—and indeed, all women. A Peeping Tom by preference, he has abandoned that dangerous activity. Now, from his private sanctuary in the basement of his home, he watches pornographic movies and makes threatening telephone calls to women, listening with intense satisfaction to their frantic pleas for help on his police scanner. To prevent his mother from discovering his illicit pastime, he has loosened the boards on the stairway as well as the handrail, actions that have already caused Mrs. Heffernan one dangerous fall. Yet so great is his hatred of his mother that Bernie feels no remorse. In fact, during the course of the novel, he conducts additional sabotage of the stairway, with painful consequences for her.

When Bernie turns his obsessive gaze on Meghan and begins stalking her, he provides the novel with one of Clark's narrative staples, the endangered heroine. Bernie's role in *I'll Be Seeing You* functions thematically as well. As the product of a hateful parent-child relationship, Bernie has been denied the sort of nurturance that Mac gives Kyle. As a result, he has failed to thrive and is, in fact, emotionally and psychologically still a child, the sad consequence of betrayal, neglect, and constant criticism. In this role, he shares some surprising affinities with Edwin Collins, Meghan's beloved father.

Meghan knows surprisingly little about her father's past, for Edwin Collins seldom shared the painful secrets of his early family life with anyone. In fact, he had constructed a fiction about his family and lived its reality. Consequently, Meghan is completely unprepared to discover among her father's papers letters from her grandmother, whom she believed had died when her father was a young boy. She is even more disturbed to learn the truth about her father's childhood, for its consequences have rippled across time and space to shape the lives of many unsuspecting victims.

When Meghan discovers her father's secret life—that he had a "wife" and a daughter living in Arizona—she searches for some explanation for his actions. She finds it in his relationship with his mother. Abandoned first as a toddler and again as an eight-year-old boy by his adored mother, the young Edwin knew little of love or security. He waited desperately for his mother to return to him and was shunted off to camp and boarding school by his father, who resented his obligations (128). By the time his mother attempted to reenter his life, the teenager had already killed her off metaphorically. For the remainder of her life, he refused to acknowledge her existence, ignoring her pleas for forgiveness and her dreams of meeting her granddaughter (66).

Although Edwin Collins learned to hide the pain of rejection and developed into a personable adult and a loving husband and father, he never truly recovered from his childhood trauma. His secret life, as Frances Grolier, her father's other "wife," explains to Meghan, was a consequence of that trauma. "On the surface," Frances tells Meghan, "Edwin had it all: charm, looks, wit, intelligence. Inwardly he was, or is, a desperately insecure man. . . . In so many ways your father was still that hurt child who feared he might be abandoned again. He needed to know he had another place to go, a place where someone would take him in" (221). Even into adulthood, Edwin Collins suffered the pain of his mother's rejection. He also struggled to secure the unquestioning love and support that rejection had denied him. He remained emotionally and psychologically a child.

Her pursuit of the truth places Meghan in a relationship with her father similar to the one he experienced with his mother. She feels his secret life as a betrayal of their trust, a rejection of her being, and suffers a profound sense of loss that undermines the foundations of her world. A self-acknowledged "Daddy's girl" (24), Meghan had adored her father and basked in his love and approval and indulgent understanding. Their relationship had been true north on her life's compass. Collins' presumed death in the Tappan Zee Bridge disaster causes Meghan to stumble on her path to success, but knowledge of his double life nearly propels her off course. Her conflicting emotions—anger, jealousy, and pity—threaten to overwhelm her native intelligence. Unlike her father, however, Meghan eventually overcomes her personal pain to forge ahead in life.

As Meghan works to clear her father's name, she also salvages part of their relationship. Despite his double life, Edwin Collins was an honest businessman, and he was, as she instinctively knew, incapable of murder. By the end of the novel, Meghan has begun to forgive her father, even if she cannot entirely understand him. At his grave, she can honestly express her love for the first man in her life.

In her focus on these parent-child relationships, Clark probes this life-giving and life-sustaining bond to indicate its power and complexity. The ideal exemplified by the MacIntyres nourishes the growth and development of a vulnerable child into a self-confident and self-reliant adult, and Meghan is herself proof of this assertion. Despite his double life, her loving father and her mother had given their daughter everything she needed to thrive, including the strength of character to overcome personal pain and adversity. The child denied such a relationship, however, must struggle to achieve adulthood, and some of these children, as the examples of Bernie Heffernan and Edwin Collins indicate, never overcome their loss. As Cyrus Graham, Edwin's step-brother, tells Meghan, "That kind of abandonment does something to the soul and the psyche" (129). It profoundly limits the child's ability to develop his or her full potential and may lead to aberrant and even criminal behavior. In all their various permutations, the parent child relationships in *I'll Be Seeing You* are the primary focus of Clark's novel, shaping both characterization and theme.

## A FEMINIST READING OF *I'LL BE SEEING YOU*

The relationship between Meghan and her father provides the feminist critic with an important analytical focus. In fact, it reveals much about the power of men to shape the lives of the women who love them. The feminist critic, as explained in Chapter 3, examines literature through the lens of gender differences and gender expectations to reveal the degree to which they define women's lives and experiences. As the first man in his daughter's life, the father exerts tremendous power, shaping her attitudes about both herself and other men. Because he is, as Lynda E. Boose notes, the "chief authorizing figure and primary model for the daughter's later male relationships," his treatment of her has a significant effect on her "relationship to the world beyond her father's house" (38). Given this perspective, the father-daughter relationships in *I'll Be Seeing You* lend a provocative subtext to Clark's primary focus.

Although Meghan shares a loving, supportive relationship with her mother, she always looked to her father for approval and self-affirmation. An indulgent father, he supplied her with the "gooey chocolate bars, marshmallows, [and] peanut brittle" that her mother forbade her as a child. Even into adulthood, he played his appropriate role. "He was the fun parent," Meghan remembers fondly. "Mother was the one who made Meghan practice the piano and make her bed." When she announced her intention to quit the law firm, it was, predictably, her mother who protested. "Daddy," she remembers, "had understood." Meghan learned early that she could depend upon her father, despite his frequent absences, and she was unabashedly a "Daddy's girl. Always" (24–25).

This tendency is one Meghan shares with her mother, who even into late adulthood reveres her father. She fears the impending loss of the Drumdoe Inn, the business she inherited from him, primarily because it will be a betrayal of all his hard work and sacrifice (232–233). Although her father is dead and she is a mature adult, Catherine Collins dreads disappointing him, a fact that suggests the conflicting legacy of the father-daughter bond. On the one hand, it develops the daughter's trust in men, but on the other, it develops her dependence upon them as well. This is certainly to some extent the case with both Catherine and Meghan Collins.

Her relationship with her father instilled in Meghan as well her sense of herself as a sexual being and her view of romantic love. To compensate for his frequent absences, her father would return home with gifts. Sometimes he would even make a "date" with his darling daughter, preparing a special meal at home for just the two of them (25) and thereby cultivating Meghan's femininity. In the course of her investigations, Meghan also recalls the dancing lessons her father gave her as a teenager. Eager to demonstrate her mastery of a jazz routine, Meghan had performed her newest steps for him. Unimpressed, her father had told her that "jazz is good music and a fine dance form, but the waltz is the dance of the angels" (202). He had then proceeded to teach her the Viennese waltz, a graceful, romantic dance from another era. He taught his daughter, in effect, to dance for him and not for herself. In this way he conveyed to her one of the realities of patriarchy: A woman must submit her will to the man she loves if she is to be loved.

A dutiful daughter eager to please Daddy and thereby retain his powerful presence in her life, Meghan is for most of the novel in psychological bondage to her father. Jeremy MacIntyre, the only man who has been able to displace her father from his central position in her life, is conveniently unavailable to her. Consequently, Meghan has not yet had to risk her father's disappointment and disapproval. Moreover, her attempt to solve the mystery surrounding his disappearance is motivated as much by her desire to redeem his name and reputation as by her need to save her mother from impending financial disaster (21). Until she sees irrefutable evidence of her father's dishonesty and betrayal in the face of her half-sister Annie, Meghan lives within her father's house. Its patriarchal structures, including the belief that father knows best, have been erected in her mind. Meghan's discovery of her father's secret life, however, fills her with knowledge that is initially life-threatening but that ultimately proves life-affirming. In fact, it frees Clark's heroine from the patriarchal prison house of male domination.

When Meghan gazes on the face of her mirror image, her half-sister Annie, she confronts a painful reality about a daughter's insignificance. As Boose observes, within the patriarchal narrative—traditional stories of men and their actions—the daughter is virtually an absence. Her temporary status within the father's house essentially denies her a name until she marries and assumes the identity of her husband (20–21). As the only child (or so she thought) of a loving father, Meghan had never had cause to feel herself an absence. Annie's reality, however, denies Meghan her special status. Not only is Annie her mirror image, she is also her namesake. Her father's two favorite names, she recalls on the day she visits Cyrus Graham and learns of her father's secret life, were Meghan and Anne, the names she herself bore. Her joy in her name, however, disappears when she learns her half-sister's name: "You got to use your two favorite names, after all, Dad, Meghan thought bitterly" (127). Meghan and Annie were interchangeable, were, in fact, replaceable. This is the bitter truth that threatens to destroy Meghan and does, in fact, result in Annie's death.

In Annie's death something dies in Meghan as well—her absolute trust in and dependence upon her father and, by extension, the men in her life. This lesson is reinforced by the duplicitous nature of so many of the men in the novel. Bernie Heffernan, the man who stalks Meghan and preys on other vulnerable women, is an obvious example. Another is Phillip Carter, her father's murderous business partner. A man who could kill the husband and then extend such concern to the widow is a particularly disgusting representative of his sex. The doctors (chiefly male) who sell babies to desperate women and exploit the bodies of other equally vulnerable women are no better than Bernie or Phillip or, for that matter, Edwin Collins. He had, after all, betrayed two wives and two daughters and thereby destroyed their worlds. Of the major male characters in *I'll Be Seeing You*, only Jeremy MacIntyre proves worthy of Meghan's trust, but only after he suffers the pain of betrayal by his wife.

In facing the truth about her father, Meghan frees herself from his well-meaning control. No longer does she depend upon his judgment and opinion. No longer does she affirm her being through his approval. Instead, she relies upon her innate intelligence and her pragmatic resourcefulness, a quality she shares with her mother, to create her presence in the world. Ultimately, Meghan simply refuses to be the victim of her father's unhappy childhood or of her own complex relationship with him. Her father was merely human, and so, after all, is she.

From any perspective, the parent-child relationships at the center of *I'll Be Seeing You* touch Clark's readers at the core of their being, for the experience of childhood is something held in common by all. We know both its joys and its sorrows, and we understand as well the parent's crucial role in shaping the experience. Lest we forget, however, Mary Higgins Clark has reminded us of the powerful legacy of this primary bond. She has reminded us, as Meghan advises Mac, that if they are to thrive, "little kids shouldn't be disappointed" (135).

# 13

# *Remember Me*
## (1994) and
# *The Anastasia Syndrome*
## (1989)

The story that became *Remember Me*, Mary Higgins Clark's eleventh bestseller, originated in the 1970s. On Cape Cod, where she has a summer home, Clark discovered a book on the region's legends and history and soon became convinced that they could provide a rich background for a novel of suspense. So she spent the next twenty years reading about the Cape's colorful history—its "mooncussers" and haunted houses, its folk chronicles and ways of life—and allowing her idea to germinate and finally bloom. As Clark notes in the acknowledgments to *Remember Me*, they are "the reason this book exists" (9).

*Remember Me* marks a departure from the sophisticated, urban settings and contemporary social problems characteristic of the novels immediately preceding it. Venturing into the realm of the gothic and the supernatural, territory she previously explored in *A Cry in the Night* (1982) and the novella *The Anastasia Syndrome* (1989), Clark created a ghost story with a contemporary edge. She wrote a psychological thriller that demonstrated the inexorable connection between the present and the past. In juxtaposing the stories of two women separated by time who are struggling to cope with the loss of a child, Clark put a new and different twist on some of her common themes and proved once again her ability to weave a haunting tale of mystery and suspense.

Menley Nichols, the heroine of *Remember Me*, has never stopped blaming herself for the death of her two-year-old son Bobby. She was, however, blameless for the accident that took his life—an oncoming train struck her car at an unguarded railroad crossing. In the aftermath of the tragedy, as she suffers from post-traumatic stress syndrome, her marriage to Adam, a high-profile criminal defense attorney, nearly falls apart. The birth of their daughter Hannah, however, revitalizes their relationship and provides them with a reason to build a future together. To begin that future, the Nicholses decide to escape the pressures of their lives in New York City by spending a month on Cape Cod, Adam's boyhood home. Soon they are living in Remember House, an eighteenth-century landmark built by a sea captain for his bride. Inspired by her surroundings, Menley, the author of a series of children's books, begins to conduct research for her next writing project. One of the most interesting legends of Cape Cod, she discovers, is the sinister tale of the house she now calls home. Built by love, Remember House was inhabited by sorrow, for, on learning of his wife's unfaithfulness, the captain had deserted her, taking with him their infant daughter. Some said that the abandoned wife and mother waited still for her daughter's return.

Soon after the Nicholses move into Remember House, the haunted past begins to assume eerie reality for Menley. A series of unexplained, and seemingly unexplainable, events casts doubt on her ability to care for Hannah. Worried about his wife's state of mind, Adam fears even more for Hannah's safety, and soon distrust and disappointment drive Menley and Adam apart once again. Menley, however, is determined to save both herself and her daughter. To do so, she must solve the mystery of Remember House before its secrets destroy her.

## GENERIC CONVENTIONS

Like *A Cry in the Night, Remember Me* owes much of its effect to Clark's use of gothic conventions (defined more fully in Chapter 6). One of those conventions is an eerie and atmospheric setting, which Remember House certainly provides. Isolated high on a bluff overlooking the ocean, the house sits "majestic" in its "starkly beautiful lines." Built in the early eighteenth century, it is "larger and more graceful" than other homes of the period, for it stands as a "tribute to the love Captain Andrew Freeman initially felt for his young bride" (33), Mehitabel. The tale of the Freemans' love forsaken, however, has filled the house with a haunted and tragic melancholy that contrasts with its architectural splendor. Its atmosphere of sadness can, in fact, work its effect on those who enter the house.

Just before the Nicholses take up residence in Remember House, Carrie Bell, a cleaning woman employed by realtor Elaine Atkins to put the property in order, gets "the fright of [her] life." The sound of footsteps draws her to an upstairs room furnished with a single bed and an antique cradle. Peering into the room, Carrie has the distinct impression that *"someone I couldn't see was sitting on the side of that bed, rocking the cradle!"* (33). Weeks later, Amy Nelson, the babysitter, is convinced that she sees Menley, dressed in a long gown, pacing Remember House's widow's walk (105). Menley, however, is conducting research in her study at the time Amy claims to have seen her. Little wonder, then, given these eerie phenomena, that Menley also has strange experiences at Remember House.

On several occasions Menley smells a musty odor when she enters the small bedroom where Carrie discovered the rocking cradle. On others, she herself finds the cradle rocking of its own volition. Even more disturbing, however, is the night Menley is awakened by the sound of a roaring train and the cries of her dead son Bobby (150–151). On other days, she awakes to find Hannah sleeping not in her crib, but in the cradle (86), or to discover Hannah's toys encircling her in her crib, an antique doll sitting in the cradle (176).

Happenings like these are conventions of the tale of gothic suspense. To create their effect, such tales rely upon unexplained events and a sinister and foreboding atmosphere, all of which are focused on a house with a haunted past. Remember House fulfills all of these demands. In fact, Menley eventually discovers its hidden rooms and secret passages and even its decayed bones, proof of the evil lurking beneath its stately facade.

Yet another gothic convention is the endangered heroine who, under the influence of the house, comes to fear for her sanity. Such is the case with Menley Nichols. Tormented by guilt about the accident that killed Bobby, Menley is still recovering from post-traumatic stress syndrome when she settles at Remember House for a summer's retreat. Consequently, the strange events that occur there work upon her fragile psyche and threaten to push her over the edge of sanity. Menley wonders, for instance, if she may have unconsciously climbed to the widow's walk. She worries, too, that while in a semi-conscious state she may have shifted Hannah from her crib to the cradle. Although she resists believing that she could have done such things, no other explanation seems possible. Soon Menley, like Adam, fears that she is losing her grip on reality and that she may be a threat to her infant daughter (95).

Like other gothic heroines, though, Menley is tough and resourceful and determined to find reasonable explanations for the mysteries in her life. While conducting research for her next book, she investigates the legends of Remember House and pursues the paranormal and occult experiences of others living on the Cape in an effort to determine their validity. She also enlists the aid of her neighbors, the Spragues, who give her the evidence she needs to solve the mysteries of Remember House.

Until Alzheimer's disease robbed her of her ability to recognize her own children or even to remember what she ate for breakfast, Phoebe Sprague was a noted professor of history at Harvard University. Prior to her impairment, Dr. Sprague had been conducting research on Remember House and had collected a thick file of documents about its original owners, the Freemans. Armed with those documents, Menley, like Phoebe before her, comes to doubt that Mehitabel Freeman was unfaithful to her husband and begins to look for alternative endings to the ancient story. Her investigations lead her to Remember House's hidden rooms and secret passages, into the dark recesses of history and memory that are the habitations of the truth. There, she faces alone the menacing forces that have been threatening her existence. She faces as well her own paralyzing guilt and fear that she may be an unfit mother. There, like the traditional gothic heroine, she restores order to her world.

The truth about Mr. Rochester's madwoman in the attic in Charlotte Brontë's *Jane Eyre* or the mysterious Rebecca of Daphne du Maurier's haunting novel lies at the heart of these classic tales of gothic suspense. Like them, *Remember Me* has a story within a story, a mystery the heroine must solve to save her own life. In fact, the story of Mehitabel Freeman runs a course parallel to Menley's own and thereby serves as a precursor to it. Three hundred years ago, Mehitabel and Andrew Freeman, like Menley and Adam Nichols, were happily married lovers driven apart by disappointment and distrust. Accused of adultery, Mehitabel was publicly beaten after her suspected lover confessed his illicit passion. Six weeks after the birth of their first child, a daughter, Andrew set sail with the infant, denying Mehitabel her only joy. Upon his departure, however, she vowed to inhabit their house until her child was returned to her (83). The sad tale, as Menley pointedly tells Adam, is about "a husband who did not trust his wife" (219), as is Menley's own story.

In her use of the story within a story, Clark not only conforms to generic convention but also resolves some of the problems that undermined a previous experiment, the novella *The Anastasia Syndrome* (1989). In that work, Judith Chase is a writer whose historical studies have earned acclaim in her dual homelands, Great Britain and the United States. Conducting research in London for her current project, a history of the English Civil War, she is also preparing for her marriage to Sir Stephen Hallett, who is expected to become Great Britain's next prime minister. Orphaned during the Second World War, Judith is also attempting to trace her origins, for, like Menley, she is suffering a type of post-traumatic stress syndrome, reliving the trauma of her separation from her mother during an air raid. In her quest, she visits Dr. Reza Patel, a renowned psychiatrist who has been conducting experiments in regression. During treatment, Judith regresses to the seventeenth century, where the spirit of Lady Margaret Carew possesses her body and soul. Lady Margaret and her family had been victims of the English Civil War, forfeiting their lives and their property to the greedy machinations of Simon Hallet. Prior to her execution, she had vowed revenge on her enemy. Judith Chase becomes the unsuspecting vehicle of that revenge.

Clark's attempt to demonstrate the interconnections between the past and the present in *The Anastasia Syndrome*, although clever, is not entirely successful, primarily because the plot is hard to believe. Unlike the concept of multiple personalities, regression to another time and possession by another person from that time are beyond the understanding of most readers. Some might be willing to suspend disbelief to entertain notions of ghosts and other supernatural manifestations. Yet those same readers would probably find it impossible to believe that an intelligent and assertive modern woman could seduce a construction worker or plant bombs in central London—even if she is possessed by the spirit of another person—without some recognition of her actions. Judith Chase does both. Clark's farfetched plot device simply cannot sustain the suspension of disbelief on which a successful tale of supernatural suspense depends.

Clark's narrative strategy also undermines *The Anastasia Syndrome*, for it is self-conscious and obtrusive. Italic type marks the shifts from Judith's story to Lady Margaret's story, drawing attention to the movement from present to past and back. Rather than allow the novella's thematic intent to evolve naturally from the interconnections between the plot and the characters of both stories, Clark chooses instead a narrative strategy that forces her point. Except for their ancestry and their possession of Edge Barton, the former Carew estate, for instance, Simon Hallet and Sir Stephen Hallett share no common traits of character. And although Judith and Lady Margaret are both strong-minded women, Judith lacks the other woman's vindictiveness. Only the manipulations and needs of plot connect these characters. Thus, Clark's narrative strategy makes it painfully obvious that we are reading two separate stories in this tale.

In *Remember Me*, Clark avoids the weaknesses of *The Anastasia Syndrome* by developing parallel stories that connect thematically but that allow the heroine her own selfhood. Menley is not possessed by Mehitabel, but rather drawn to her by the similarities between their stories, by her shared feelings for another mother unjustly condemned. Mehitabel's story is revealed as a natural consequence of Menley's fascination with it and her need to know it. It is not imposed on Menley's story, as Lady Margaret's is imposed on Judith's. Finally, the supernatural elements of *Remember Me* bear sufficient connection to natural phenomena to be believable. Consequently, even the novel's coincidences, including the final one that establishes a true link between Menley and Mehitabel, seem within the realm of possibility. Ultimately, Clark's assured handling of the gothic conventions gives coherence to *Remember Me*'s narrative elements and creates a satisfying tale of mystery and suspense.

## THEMATIC ISSUES

In its thematic concerns, *Remember Me* travels familiar paths, thereby more clearly defining the issues that prompt Clark to spin her tales. From the beginning of her career Clark has focused on the interconnections between the past and the present, and that theme is central to *Remember Me*. In this novel the ghostly presence of Mehitabel Freeman that haunts Remember House makes possible Elaine Atkins' plot against Menley. Determined to possess Adam, his old friend and confidante preys upon Menley's fragile psyche, creating, with the help of Scott Covey, the cruel phenomena that drive Menley to the brink of insanity. Similarly, it is her investigations into the past that help Menley solve the mystery of Remember House.

The trope of memory, a repeated pattern of references that figures so prominently in the novel, also emphasizes the connections between the past and the present. Remember House, like the mind, is the repository of memory. Its name refers not simply to a structure, but to a person, for Remember was the name given to the child born to the Freemans. Thus it evokes an old legend of yet another woman who, knowing that she would die in childbirth, directed that her baby be named Remember "so it would always remember her" (254). Memory links us to the past and connects us to lives beyond our own. To be forgotten or to forget is a source of emotional pain and psychological unease. Certainly this point lies behind Clark's inclusion of Phoebe Sprague, who suffers from Alzheimer's disease and whose life and very being have been profoundly diminished as a consequence of her inability to remember. Clark's grounding of the novel in yet another disease of memory, post-traumatic stress syndrome, however, speaks most directly to this theme and connects it as well to another common concern, the need to face the past to be free from it.

Although more than two years have passed since the train accident that took her son's life, Menley has been unable to accept her blamelessness in the incident. Neither has she entirely accepted the loss of her son. The birth of her daughter Hannah should have provided a reason to move forward with her life. It triggers instead the old guilt, and as a consequence, she relives the accident over and over in her mind, as if to revise its horrific ending or to punish herself for her failures. Post-traumatic stress syndrome keeps raw and bleeding the pain of the past, and treatment has failed to heal her wounds.

Menley herself is the only one capable of mending her battered psyche, and to do so, she must accept her loss and grieve. This healing process begins on the day that Menley vows to fight her involuntary commitment to a psychiatric facility (223). She vows to fight, in other words, to keep her daughter. The healing is nearly completed the day Menley watches a videotape of Bobby with a mixture of sorrow and joy that yields understanding. She knows that the pain of her loss will never entirely subside. Yet she has also recognized, as she tells Amy, that "you learn to be grateful that you had the person at all, even though it wasn't long enough" (273). Like so many of Clark's heroines, Menley has found the key to the future by opening the door to her past.

The parent-child relationship is another recurrent theme in *Remember Me*, and here Clark uses subplots to great effect. Graham and Anne Carpenter are the focus of one subplot. Their daughter Vivian recently drowned under suspicious circumstances, three months after marrying an impoverished actor who now stands to inherit her fortune. Vivian's death has left her parents both heartsick and guilt-ridden. Their relationship with their daughter had always been a troubled one, and now they wonder to what extent they are responsible for her death. Born late in their marriage, when her parents were eager to live their own lives, Vivian had been "a demanding, malcontent child who became a problem teenager and a difficult adult." Her father worries that "her lifelong hostility to them and insecurity with others [had been] triggered in the womb" by an instinctual understanding that she was "unwanted" (48). Her mother acknowledges to herself that "none of us loved her the way she needed to be loved" (112). Like Menley, they blame themselves unnecessarily for the loss of their child. Nevertheless, they accept the parents' responsibility to love and to nurture their child even into adulthood. They also know that in some crucial and essential way they failed Vivian as parents and that their failure made her vulnerable to the superficial charms of Scott Covey. To some extent, in other words, they are responsible for the loss of their daughter, but they had lost her even before she died.

Amy and John Nelson are the focus of another parent-child relationship in *Remember Me*. Like the Carpenters', its troubled nature exposes the difficulty of balancing the needs of parents with those of the child. On the verge of adulthood, eighteen-year-old Amy wants only the best for the father who has played the role of both parents since the death of her mother six years before. She knows that she should be pleased that he has become engaged to Elaine Atkins, but she is not. Sensing Amy's dislike of Elaine, Menley fears that it is selfishly motivated. She remembers her own brother's attempts to destroy their mother's relationships with other men following the death of their father (76) and believes that Amy may be playing a similar game.

Amy, however, cannot help but compare Elaine unfavorably to her own mother, who was "real." Unlike Elaine, who laughs at his "long-winded stories" as if he were "Robin Williams or something" (169), her mother would quietly and affectionately prevent her father from making a fool of himself. Moreover, John Nelson, as Amy tells Menley, may be "nice and kind and good and successful," but he is also "a very boring man" whom Elaine does not love. In fact, Amy confesses to Menley, Elaine is "going to make him miserable and she knows that I know it and that's why she can't stand me" (262).

Within the context of Clark's ongoing exploration of the parent-child relationship, these two examples demonstrate once again both its importance and its complexity. Clearly, the child never outgrows his or her need for the parent, even when the relationship is strained. Furthermore, the parent remains forever a parent, connected to the child by ties of blood and memory that surpass understanding. The Carpenters' guilt about their daughter's death, Amy's concern for her father, Menley's fear of separation from her child, Mehitabel's grief for her infant daughter—in *Remember Me*, all are proof of those ties.

## A FEMINIST READING OF *REMEMBER ME*

Clark's emphasis upon the parent-child relationship provides the feminist critic with some provocative avenues of exploration, particularly in *Remember Me*, where the specter of an unfit mother haunts the lives of the novel's heroine and her double. Examining literature from the perspective of gender differences and gender expectations, the feminist critic would focus especially on the ideal of motherhood central to the novel. Mothering has traditionally been the exclusive prerogative of women, viewed almost as a biological obligation or necessity. Moreover, motherhood has traditionally defined half of a woman's role (the role of wife being the other half). While the woman who never becomes a mother is frequently considered only half a woman, the woman who proves herself unfit for motherhood is regarded as a complete failure as a woman and as a human being. Thus, the specter of the unfit mother that haunts both Menley and Mehitabel cuts to the very core of their being and threatens to destroy both.

When Menley hears the sad story of Mehitabel Freeman, she knows instinctively that something about it rings false. Nearly three hundred years before Menley's own story begins, Andrew Freeman deemed his wife an unfit mother and separated her from her infant daughter. Accused of adultery, Mehitabel, three months pregnant with her first child, had protested her innocence. But not even her husband would believe the word of a mere woman, especially when her suspected lover confessed his guilt. Consumed by grief for her lost child, Mehitabel died having vowed to inhabit her home until she was reunited with her daughter. To Menley's mind, this response to her situation is evidence not of an unfit mother, but of a woman utterly committed to motherhood, as Menley is herself.

The author of a successful series of children's books, Menley clearly understands and relates to her audience. Furthermore, she is, by Adam's own account, "a natural homemaker" capable of "effortlessly" creating "an inviting atmosphere" (194) wherever she lives. She was and is, moreover, a devoted mother. In fact, "nothing had prepared her," she realizes, "for the torrents of love she'd felt when Bobby was born and that were evoked now by" Hannah (23). Robbed by a tragic accident of her child and, by extension, a part of herself, she feels deeply Adam's constant surveillance of her mothering, his silent accusation of unfitness. She fears that his fears may rob her once again of her child.

Unjustly accused, Menley identifies instinctively with Mehitabel, another falsely accused mother, so she begins to investigate *her* story, not history. History, as Menley knows, tells only half the tale, the half of those empowered by position and by gender to recite their story and to be believed. History, in other words, tells the stories of men. Women, from their subordinate positions as wives and mothers, have been largely silenced. Mehitabel was once silenced, but now Menley determines to give her voice. "I want to tell Mehitabel's story" (175), she acknowledges to herself, because to tell her story may be to avoid her fate. If she can prove Mehitabel unjustly accused, perhaps she can convince Adam of his own false accusations, of her own fitness to mother.

Her bout with post-traumatic stress syndrome does provide some reason for genuine concern about Menley's state of mind and thus her ability to care for Hannah. Nobody, however, ever questions Adam's ability do so. He is, after all, the man of the house, the father in a male-dominated society that believes that father knows best. He clearly loves his daughter, so he must, by extension, be a capable and responsible parent. Yet as a father, Adam is certainly not above reproach.

Although his presence may not have prevented the tragic accident that killed their son, Adam was not with Menley on the day the train rammed their car. He was keeping "a long-standing golf date" (219) instead of joining his wife and child for a visit with friends. Several years later, Adam is often absent from his family during the month they intended to spend together. Although he takes up Scott Covey's defense at Menley's urging, the high-profile lawyer frequently finds himself called to New York to oversee other legal cases. Business often takes precedence over family. Given Adam's concern for Menley's sanity and Hannah's safety, this choice seems especially irresponsible. Within a patriarchal society, however, Adam is merely performing his proper role. Thus, because he functions within the bounds of that role, his ability to parent—to do more than pat his child on the back or tuck her into bed at night—is simply assumed.

Within this context, Menley's struggle is as much about overcoming self-doubt and asserting her own being as it is about proving her fitness for motherhood, and eventually she does both. Her guilt about Bobby's death is understandable. Her jealousy about Elaine is less so unless viewed as evidence of an essential insecurity, which is exactly what it is. Years after their marriage, Menley still cannot quite believe that from "a string of girlfriends" (38) Adam chose her (238). Recalling her grandmother's belief that in marriage "it's better if the woman . . . doesn't love as deeply" (38), she worries, too, that she loves Adam too much, more, in fact, than he loves her. Indeed, she fears that her love makes her vulnerable.

Eventually, however, Menley seizes control of her situation. When she tells her husband, "Adam, I know myself" (219), she announces her recovery of self. She also puts Adam on notice that she will no longer tolerate his doubt and distrust, no longer allow them to undermine her sense of self. She tells her therapist, in fact, that there may soon come a time when, her husband having failed her, she will "neither need nor want him" (223). From the position of power that her self-assurance affords her, Menley vows to fight Adam's plan to commit her to a psychiatric facility (223). She also makes clear that she will permit nobody to separate her from her child. Menley Nichols is indeed a fit mother because she is ultimately a fit person.

By the end of *Remember Me*, Menley has told Mehitabel's story and recovered her own. She has faced the past in order to avoid her double's fate and to create the ending she has always wanted—a happy family in a happy home (64), and she has found that home at Remember House. Menley has indeed come home.

# 14

# *Let Me Call You Sweetheart*
## (1995)

The death of a beautiful woman, according to Edgar Allan Poe, is a source of deep emotion and great poetry. For Mary Higgins Clark, it is also the inspiration for her twelfth best-selling novel of mystery and suspense, *Let Me Call You Sweetheart*. The brutal murder of Suzanne Reardon in the Sweetheart Murder Case, nearly eleven years before the events in the novel, lies at the heart of this complex tale of obsessive love and betrayal. It provides Clark with the opportunity to explore and expand several of her recurrent themes, including the nature of true beauty and the bond between parent and child. It also allows her to demonstrate the degree to which a callous disregard for others diminishes us all.

Although Skip Reardon, the man convicted in the Sweetheart Murder Case, sits in prison protesting his innocence, prosecutor Kerry McGrath, the heroine of *Let Me Call You Sweetheart*, believes that justice has been served. At trial, Skip Reardon's defense attorney may have been inept, but Frank Green's prosecution of the case had been brilliant, and a jury of Reardon's peers had weighed the evidence and found him guilty of the murder of his wife, Suzanne. Geoffrey Dorso, however, the lawyer who is now conducting Reardon's appeal for a new trial, believes in his client's innocence, and eventually, circumstances lead Kerry to doubt the original verdict.

When Kerry's daughter, Robin, is injured in an automobile accident, suffering superficial but potentially disfiguring cuts to her face, she is treated by a plastic surgeon, Dr. Charles Smith. A week after the accident, as Kerry waits in his office for Robin, who is having her stitches removed, the face of a strikingly beautiful woman captures her interest. She thinks that surely she knows her from somewhere, but when Smith's nurse reveals the woman's name, it means nothing to Kerry. Her face, however, haunts Kerry's memory, and then, on her next visit to Smith's office, it becomes a reality again—but this time on a different woman. Dr. Smith, it appears, is re-creating the same face on many of his patients, and that face, as Kerry comes to realize, is the face of the Sweetheart Murder victim.

Intrigued by what certainly must be more than coincidence, Kerry begins to investigate Skip Reardon's story and Smith's connection to the murder. Her inquiries soon place her in conflict with both friends and associates, none of whom is eager to see the case reopened. They also jeopardize a coveted appointment to the New Jersey judiciary. They even lead to threats against Robin's life. Clearly, the Sweetheart Murder Case is far from closed, and every clue that Kerry uncovers brings her closer to the truth—and to death.

## GENERIC CONVENTIONS OF MYSTERY AND SUSPENSE

Although Clark has made her reputation as the "Queen of Suspense," *Let Me Call You Sweetheart* is primarily a mystery, and a cleverly crafted one at that. As a tale of secrets revealed, the mystery relies on certain established conventions of plot development for its effect. Chief among them are a cast of characters with both the motive and the means to commit a crime and the presentation of clues that make it possible for readers to match wits with the detective and solve the crime before all is revealed. To frustrate their efforts, mystery writers often include a number of red herrings, or false clues, that are intended to divert suspicion from the real villain and lead readers down dead ends. Clark makes use of all of these conventions in *Let Me Call You Sweetheart*. In fact, she even turns one of her standard techniques—exploration of the killer's mind—into a red herring, adding a special twist for those familiar with her work.

Clark assembles a diverse group of suspects in *Let Me Call You Sweetheart* and then casts suspicion on them all. Chief among them is Dr. Charles Smith, the plastic surgeon who is replicating the murder victim's beautiful face. Smith, Kerry soon discovers, was the father of Suzanne Reardon. He had also been the principal witness against his son-in-law, testifying that Skip Reardon was prone to jealous rages and contradicting Reardon's claims that another man had been giving Suzanne jewelry that was now missing. Given Smith's obsessive behavior regarding his daughter, Kerry begins to doubt the truth of the surgeon's statements and his motives for making them.

Two additional suspects are also implicated in the case. James "Jimmy" Weeks had been Suzanne's secret lover. In fact, on the day of her death it was he who had sent to Suzanne the sweetheart roses that were found strewn across her lifeless body. Weeks, a reputed crime boss, is now facing charges of income tax evasion in federal court. The last thing he needs is his connection to the Sweetheart Murder Case to become public knowledge, but Kerry, who is coming dangerously close to the truth, appears bent on making it happen.

Jason Arnott also has reason to fear the reopening of the Sweetheart Murder Case, for he had been in the Reardon home on the night of the murder—intent on stealing several pieces of Suzanne's costly jewelry. This debonair connoisseur of fine antiques and rare art objects moves in the most exclusive social circles, where his witty conversation is a valued commodity. Access to the homes of the privileged provides Arnott with the opportunity to survey their owners' treasures. Eventually he returns, an uninvited guest, to steal the most exquisite of those items and secrete them in his private collection in his Catskill Mountain mansion. Just such an errand had drawn him to the home of Suzanne Reardon on the night of her murder. Now he fears that further investigation of the case will expose his knowledge of the crime and also his clandestine occupation.

Any one of these characters could be Suzanne's killer, the man whose voice readers "hear" in the opening sequence of the novel. That sequence, which takes readers into the mind of the killer, is one of Clark's typical narrative strategies. It establishes the villain's existence and his intent to harm the heroine. It also provides some insight into his motives and moral character. Readers learn in this sequence, for instance, that ten years after the murder the killer is still haunted by his memory of Suzanne, obsessed by her beauty and the enigma of her personality. He is also determined to prevent Kerry from exposing him.

Generally Clark relies extensively on such sequences, using them to reveal crucial information and to raise the level of suspense at appropriate intervals. In *Let Me Call You Sweetheart*, however, Clark limits her readers' exposure to the criminal's mind and thereby keeps his identity shrouded in mystery. Moreover, in this novel, the sequence is so general that it provides absolutely no clue to the killer's identity. If anything, it serves almost as a red herring, for when the killer is revealed, he is such an unlikely subject that it seems impossible such thoughts could have been his. From Jimmy Weeks or Charles Smith, obsessive love and murderous intent seem entirely plausible. But the real killer, State Senator Jonathan Hoover, is such a respected citizen, such a cultured gentleman, and such a devoted benefactor to Kerry that commission of such a heinous crime seems entirely out of character.

Such a surprise is a tribute to Clark's ability to provide readers with the clues to solve the mystery, including knowledge of the crucial piece of jewelry that links Hoover to the crime, and also to lead them down false trails, as she does with the bouquet of sweetheart roses. Clark does violate to some extent the rules of fair play in a mystery by not divulging until the novel's end Hoover's acquaintance with Suzanne, and thereby increasing the readers' difficulty in solving the case. But the presentation of clues is so unobtrusive, the cast of suspects so believable, the weaving together of the plot's various threads so seamless, that Clark demonstrates, as Marilyn Stasio claims, that her "technique isn't all a bag of tricks" (24).

Eventually, Clark does crank up the novel's level of suspense, and when she does, she relies on her standard techniques for creating it. Kerry's investigation of the Sweetheart Murder Case takes place against the backdrop of the prosecution of Jimmy Weeks in federal court, proceedings that are rapidly drawing to a conclusion, and the governor's imminent announcement of judicial appointments. Both lend a sense of urgency to her quest because they threaten her life and her livelihood. To dissuade her from her pursuit of the truth, Weeks has launched a campaign of intimidation against Kerry through her daughter, and the governor threatens to withhold her nomination to the bench. When neither tactic works, both Kerry and Robin find themselves confronting death in the novel's climactic scene, and as always, Clark's endangered heroine escapes its clutches—but not before readers experience some anxiety of their own. As Stasio notes, Clark may write "to a simple formula," but she "taps into some elemental fear that really gives you the willies" (24).

## THEMATIC ISSUES

Character development in *Let Me Call You Sweetheart* is largely subsumed in thematic issues. Clark's heroine, Kerry McGrath, is a successful professional in her mid-thirties whose reputation as a "smart, tough, and scrupulous lawyer" (31) has already placed her in line for a judicial seat. She is one of Clark's typical heroines, as strong and resourceful as Katie DeMaio, Pat Traymore, or Meghan Collins. Divorced from Bob Kinellen, Kerry is a devoted mother to ten-year-old Robin, treating her with a warm mixture of sympathy and respect that nurtures her daughter's own developing personality. So strong are her sense of self and her moral principles that she refuses to be intimidated by all those who warn her away from the case. Kerry's resolve may waver when her coveted judgeship is jeopardized and bend when Robin's life is threatened, but it never breaks. From beginning to end, Kerry stands firm for all the principles that Clark champions in the novel. Those principles Clark makes clear as she develops the themes of *Let Me Call You Sweetheart*.

The ideal of justice, a theme that Clark had previously explored in *A Stranger Is Watching* (1978), figures prominently in this novel by virtue of Kerry's quest for the truth in the Sweetheart Murder Case. If, as he maintains, Skip Reardon did not murder his wife, then an innocent man has been imprisoned for ten years and a terrible injustice has been done to him. As a prosecuting attorney, Kerry is committed to seek the truth, so she is deeply troubled by Reardon's situation. She is equally distressed by the willingness of others, especially those charged with upholding the law, to protect themselves at the expense of an innocent man. Frank Green, for instance, Kerry's boss, secured his reputation prosecuting the case, but now risks the gubernatorial nomination should it be reopened, and State Senator Jonathan Hoover is equally intent on playing politics with another man's life. He is determined to manipulate the gubernatorial election to achieve his own political ends.

Justice compromised, however, compromises everyone, as the situation of Kerry's ex-husband, Bob Kinellen, illustrates. Ten years before, Kerry and Bob had divorced when he joined a law firm known for representing wealthy but disreputable clients and she realized that he was not the man she thought he was. Now, Kinellen, who is defending Jimmy Weeks, is willfully ignoring the implications of his client's confidence in a verdict of innocence. He suspects that Weeks is tampering with the jury and threatening witnesses, but by choosing not to openly challenge his client about his actions, he hopes to avoid being implicated himself in Weeks' illegalities. But when Weeks forces him to deliver to Kerry the threat against his own daughter's life, Kinellen learns the consequences of moral compromise. As Kerry had warned him at the time of their divorce, "Lie down with dogs and you'll get up with fleas" (181).

In her pursuit of truth and justice, even Kerry wavers in her resolve,

standing firm on principle when only her judgeship is at risk but seriously reconsidering her position, and understandably so, perhaps, when
her daughter's life is threatened. Yet as Robin reminds her mother, who
has just criticized her father for justifying illegal actions but is now ready
to abandon her investigation to protect her daughter, "That's totally unfair. You're putting Dad down for something, and then you're doing the
same thing. Isn't *not* helping Geoff if you think his client shouldn't be
in prison 'situational ethics'?" (207). Robin's question gets to the heart
of the complex moral issues that Clark explores in her novel and makes
clear her perspective on them. As difficult as her choice may be, Kerry
must do the right thing, and when she does, the justness of her actions
leads to justice for all—Skip Reardon's innocence is proven, Robin's life
is saved, and the Sweetheart murderer finally pays for his crime.

*Let Me Call You Sweetheart* develops another recurrent Clark theme, the
nature of true beauty, through the actions of two characters, Dr. Charles
Smith and Jason Arnott, both of whom value physical perfection over
all other moral or spiritual qualities. Arnott, the gentleman cat burglar,
simply cannot resist the Aubusson carpets and Fabergé desk seals owned
by others who, he believes, are incapable of valuing their beauty. Convinced that his aesthetic sense is superior to others', Arnott feels justified
in stealing their beautiful objects and securing them in his private collection, where they will be truly appreciated. "Beauty," he thinks, "made
[me] do those things" (123), and in truth, beauty has made a thief of
him. It has even made him a murderer. Clearly, there is nothing enno-
bling about his pursuit of beautiful objects rather than an ideal of beauty.

Dr. Charles Smith has been guilty of similar objectification in pursuit
of beauty, with equally reprehensible results. He possesses the ability to
"wrest" beauty "from bone and muscle and flesh" (269), and thus he
fancies himself an artist (182). Given the raw materials—women with
good bone structure and the willingness to submit to his vision of
them—Smith creates and re-creates his ideal of physical perfection, the
petulant, sexually provocative beauty that he had sculpted in his daughter Suzanne. Beneficiaries of Smith's gift, however, eventually learn its
cost: They must include him in their lives. Obsessed by his creations,
Smith believes that he should "be allowed to take pleasure" in them.
"Why," he wonders, "should the creation be wasted among leering
dregs of humanity while the artist suffers for a glimpse of it?" (182). Too
late, Suzanne learns her obligation, and the same is true of Barbara
Tompkins, whom Smith begins to stalk following her transforming surgery.

Smith's obsession with his creations clearly evokes the Greek myth of Pygmalion. In the myth, Pygmalion, King of Cyprus, found so much to blame in women that he came to despise their sex and resolved never to marry. He did, however, love beauty, so he sculpted from ivory a female figure of such physical perfection that he fell in love with his creation. Moved by his depth of passion, Aphrodite, the goddess of love, breathed life into the figure to create the perfect union of physical and spiritual beauty through love.

Like Pygmalion, Smith, too, despises women, but worships the physical perfection he has created. He treats his daughter, for instance, with "reverence" (83), as if she were a museum piece. Unlike the mythological king, however, Smith's obsession is to possess his beauties, not love them. As Jason Arnott tells Kerry, "Smith would have built a guardrail around [Suzanne] to keep others away from her, pretty much the way museums put guardrails around their most precious objects" (225).

Ultimately, what motivates both Arnott and Smith is their own selfishness, their desire to possess outward beauty, for neither is capable of appreciating inner beauty. Both took delight in Suzanne Reardon, a woman who by all accounts flirted shamelessly with every man she met and treated others, including her husband, with contempt. Yet neither recognizes the nobility of character that animates and transforms even the humblest and homeliest into a pleasing shape. Such beauty is revealed in the loyalty of Beth Taylor, the woman Skip Reardon jilted to marry Suzanne, the woman who so believes in his innocence that she has never married and continues to wait for the man she loves. It is evident in the love Kerry shares with her daughter and the strength of character that motivates her every action. And it is clear in the sacrifice that Grace Hoover, a woman crippled by arthritis, makes when she shoots her beloved husband to thwart his evil intent to kill Kerry and Robin. The beauty of such actions is beyond the understanding of those who cannot penetrate pleasing surfaces.

## A FEMINIST PERSPECTIVE ON *LET ME CALL YOU SWEETHEART*

The parent-child relationships in *Let Me Call You Sweetheart* also highlight the continuing importance of this thematic subject in Clark's fiction. They yield some provocative insights into the development of a woman's sense of self when viewed from the perspective of the feminist critic.

Such a critique, which is detailed in Chapter 3, examines the degree to which gender roles and gender expectations are reflected in the literary text and focuses particularly in this novel on the crucial father-daughter relationship as a reflection of patriarchy's betrayal of women.

In a patriarchal society, male authority is virtually unchallenged. Men, who are the leaders of governments and other civic, commercial, and legal institutions, the heads of religious groups and family structures, by virtue of their interaction with the larger world outside the home, develop an understanding of and perspective on life's complexities which justify their role as chief decision-maker. Confined to their domestic sphere, women, in contrast, must rely on the benevolent guidance and protection of the men in their lives, and they must defer to their superior judgments.

As the first man in his daughter's life, the father wields tremendous power over her. Eager to please, the daughter looks to his judgments for self-affirmation, and his view of her shapes her subsequent relations with the other men in her life, especially those she loves. In the family, the father also represents to his daughter the gender roles appropriate to his culture. Conversely, his actions in the microcosmic family unit provide evidence of cultural attitudes and values. In *Let Me Call You Sweetheart*, that evidence indicates that a patriarchal structure harms the women it intends to protect.

The most obvious example of this consequence lies in the relationship between Suzanne Reardon and her father. When her parents divorced shortly after her birth, Suzanne was raised by her mother and adopted by her stepfather. For more than fifteen years she had virtually no contact with her biological father, and when she did go to live with him following her mother's death, she soon realized that she was a great disappointment to him. A homely and unhappy girl lacking in self-confidence, Suzanne eagerly allowed her father to transform her into a stunning beauty who was the object of every man's, including her father's, adoration. In his response to his daughter, Smith had, in effect, confirmed her previous understanding of the world—that only the beautiful were worthy of love. Such a view, of course, denies the importance of wit and intelligence, of loyalty and compassion, of any other inner qualities that define a woman's separate sense of self, and thus undermines both her authority and autonomy. It is a profound betrayal of her very being.

To a lesser degree, Robin Kinellen experiences a similar denial because her father keeps her on the periphery of his life. Although Bob Kinellen may love the daughter who clearly adores him, he has very little time to devote to her. In fact, more often than not, he cancels their plans to be together. Moreover, her stepmother resents the child of her husband's marriage to Kerry McGrath and seldom includes her in family activities with her father and stepbrothers. Consequently, Kinellen arranges to see Robin when his wife is out of town. Throughout the novel, Bob Kinellen has the power to light up his daughter's life at the mere prospect of seeing him and to extinguish that flame with every cancellation. Yet Robin never loses faith in him, and she never ceases trying to please him and thereby gaining a place in his life. Kinellen's benign neglect thus instills in his daughter one of the truths of patriarchy—the subordinate status of women. His complicity in the threats against her reinforces that truth, if not for Robin, then at least for Clark's readers. In fact, it even suggests that women are expendable.

Kerry's experience also illustrates the duplicitous nature of paternalism. Following her father's death and her mother's remarriage and relocation to Colorado, Kerry found a surrogate father in Hoover. He was the benevolent guardian of her happiness and the supportive benefactor of her career. But when Hoover violates her trust and threatens her and Robin's lives, Kerry suffers the ultimate patriarchal betrayal. This "father" is more than willing to sacrifice his "daughter" to save himself, and thus, the patriarchal myth is exposed as a lie. Kerry must trust in and rely upon herself, not the men in her life, if she is to prevail.

Clark's subtle critique of patriarchy is underscored by the warm and supportive relationship that Kerry shares with her daughter. Like her ex-husband, Kerry is also a busy lawyer with many demands on her time, but she makes every effort to be there for Robin. She genuinely listens to her daughter's confidences and respects her viewpoints, and in doing so, she nurtures Robin's developing sense of self and validates her autonomy.

The key to the mystery of the Sweetheart Murder Case is an antique pin of a flower connected by a silver chain to a bud—"the momma and the baby," Grace Hoover had called it (310). That pin symbolizes the ideal parent-child relationship, the type that allows the bud to blossom, that gives the child the opportunity to become what she can be. In *Let Me Call You Sweetheart*, that ideal is presented in a maternal, not a paternal, relationship, in a mother's unselfish love of and willingness to sacrifice herself for her child. It is presented in the relationship between Kerry and Robin.

Kerry's selflessness ultimately exposes the selfishness that leads to deceit and murder, that compromises honor and justice, that denies autonomy and authority to the individual. In exposing the destructiveness of this human weakness, Clark makes a powerful statement about contemporary society and takes a firm moral stance. They are the true solution to the Sweetheart Murder Case.

# Bibliography

*Note*: Page numbers referred to in the text are to the paperback editions of Mary Higgins Clark's novels, with the exception of the following. *Remember Me*, *The Lottery Winner*, and *Let Me Call You Sweetheart*. These page references are to the hardcover editions of the books. References in the text to *Loves Music, Loves to Dance*, interview, refer to the paperback edition in which the interview appeared.

## WORKS BY MARY HIGGINS CLARK

*All Around the Town*. New York: Simon and Schuster, 1992; Pocket Books, 1993.
"Always a Storyteller." *The Writer*, August 1987: 9–11.
*The Anastasia Syndrome and Other Stories*. New York: Simon and Schuster, 1989; Pocket Books, 1991.
*Aspire to the Heavens: A Portrait of George Washington*. New York: Meredith Press, 1969.
*The Cradle Will Fall*. New York: Simon and Schuster, 1980; Pocket Books, 1991.
*A Cry in the Night*. New York: Simon and Schuster, 1982; Pocket Books, 1993.
*I'll Be Seeing You*. New York: Simon and Schuster, 1993; Pocket Books, 1994.
*Let Me Call You Sweetheart*. New York: Simon and Schuster, 1995.
*The Lottery Winner: Alvirah and Willy Stories*. New York: Simon and Schuster, 1994.
*Loves Music, Loves to Dance*. New York: Simon and Schuster, 1991; Pocket Books, 1992.
*Remember Me*. New York: Simon and Schuster, 1994.

*Stillwatch*. New York: Simon and Schuster, 1984; Dell, 1988.
*A Stranger Is Watching*. New York: Simon and Schuster, 1978; Dell, 1988.
"Suspense Writing." *The Writer*, September 1980: 9–12.
"Taking the Plunge." *The Writer*, July 1992: 5–6.
*Weep No More, My Lady*. New York: Simon and Schuster, 1987; Dell, 1988.
*Where Are the Children?* New York: Simon and Schuster, 1975; Pocket Books, 1992.
*While My Pretty One Sleeps*. New York: Simon and Schuster, 1989; Pocket Books,
     1990.

## WORKS ABOUT MARY HIGGINS CLARK

Coiner, Jill Brooke. "She Dunnit!" *Family Circle*, 22 December 1992, 60–63.
Conroy, Sarah Booth. "The Family Plots." *Washington Post*, 28 September 1993:
     C1, C4.
Donohue, John W. "Of Many Things." *America*, 1 May 1993: 2.
Fakih, Kimberly Olson. "The Reassuring Triumph of the Good: An Interview
     with Mary Higgins Clark." *Library Journal*, 15 March 1990: 35–37.
Freeman, Lucy. "Mary Higgins Clark." *Armchair Detective* 18, 3 (1985): 228–237.
Hoch, Edward D. "Clark, Mary Higgins." In *Twentieth Century Crime and Mys-
     tery Writers*. 3rd ed. Ed. Lesley Henderson. Chicago: St. James, 1991:
     210–211.
Hoopes, Roy. "Shedunnit." *Modern Maturity*, August-September 1989: 52–57.
Kopecky, Gini. "The Way We Were." *Redbook*, March 1991: 101–108.
Lipton, Michael A., and Ann Guerin. "Murders, They Write." *People Weekly*, 2
     November 1992: 79–82.
Mitgang, Herbert. "Mary Higgins Clark." *New York Times Book Review*, 14 May
     1978: 52.
O'Brien, Maureen. "Mary Higgins Clark Lands $35 Million Deal with S & S."
     *Publishers Weekly*, 19 October 1992: 9.
O'Neill, Elizabeth Hill. "PW Interviews: Mary Higgins Clark." *Publishers Weekly*,
     19 May 1989: 64–65.
Swanson, Jean, and Dean James. "Clark, Mary Higgins." In *By a Woman's Hand:
     A Guide to Mystery Fiction by Women*. New York: Berkeley Books, 1994: 45–
     46.
Whissen, Thomas. "Mary Higgins Clark." In *Great Women Mystery Writers: Classic
     to Contemporary*. Ed. Kathleen Gregory Klein. Westport, Conn.: Greenwood
     Press, 1994: 66–69.

## INTERVIEWS WITH MARY HIGGINS CLARK

Mary Higgins Clark, interviewed by the author, 12 December 1994. New York,
     NY.
Mary Higgins Clark, "An Interview with Mary Higgins Clark." In *Loves Music,
     Loves to Dance*, unpaginated. New York: Pocket Books, 1992.

## REVIEWS AND CRITICISM

### *Where Are the Children?*

*Best Sellers*, November 1975: 237.
*Booklist*, 1 April 1975: 808.
*Journal of Reading*, 22 (1978): 127.
*Kirkus Reviews*, 1 January 1975: 39.
*Library Journal*, 1 March 1975: 506.
*Publishers Weekly*, 16 June 1975: 74.
*Publishers Weekly*, 8 March 1976: 69.
*Voice of Youth Advocates*, December 1983: 265.

### *A Stranger Is Watching*

*Best Sellers*, March 1978: 377.
*Booklist*, 15 March 1978: 1164.
*English Journal*, 68 (1979): 80.
*Kirkus Reviews*, 15 December 1977: 1331.
*Library Journal*, 1 March 1978: 589.
*Observer* (London), 7 May 1978: 34.
*Progressive*, May 1978: 45.
*Publishers Weekly*, 26 December 1977: 59.
*Publishers Weekly*, 15 January 1979: 130.
*Spectator*, 19 August 1978: 22.
*Wilson Library Bulletin*, June 1978: 801.

### *The Cradle Will Fall*

*Best Sellers*, September 1980: 196.
*Booklist*, 1 June 1980: 1109.
Clemons, Walter. "Cool Books for Hot Days." *Newsweek*, 30 June 1980: 65.
*English Journal*, 71 (1982): 81.
*Kirkus Reviews*, 1 March 1980: 303.
*Library Journal*, 1 April 1980: 883.
*New Yorker*, 4 August 1980: 92.
*Observer* (London), 5 October 1980: 28.
*Publishers Weekly*, 20 March 1980: 44.
*Publishers Weekly*, 17 April 1981: 61.
*School Library Journal*, September 1980: 90.

## *A Cry in the Night*

*Best Sellers*, December 1982: 331.
*Booklist*, 1 September 1982: 1.
Jakab, Elisabeth. "Suspense Story." *New York Times Book Review*, 14 November
    1982: 15.
*Kirkus Reviews*, 15 July 1982: 809.
*Library Journal*, 15 September 1982: 1768.
*Publishers Weekly*, 30 July 1982: 62.
*Publishers Weekly*, 12 August 1983: 64.
*School Library Journal*, January 1983: 90.
*West Coast Review of Books*, November 1982: 33.


## *Stillwatch*

*American Spectator*, December 1984: 26.
*Best Sellers*, December 1984: 322.
*Booklist*, 1 October 1984: 146.
*Kirkus Reviews*, 15 August 1984: 762.
*Los Angeles Times Book Review*, 4 November 1984: 11.
*Publishers Weekly*, 7 September 1984: 70.
Simpson, Mona. Review of *Stillwatch*. *New York Times Book Review*, 9 December
    1984: 11.
Stoll, Jeffrey E. "A Novelist Looks at the Death Penalty." *New York Times*, 9 July
    1978. Sec. 11, 20.
*West Coast Review of Books*, March 1985: 30.


## *Weep No More, My Lady*

*Booklist*, 1 May 1987: 1314.
*Chicago Tribune Books*, 12 June 1988: 5.
*Christian Science Monitor*, 19 August 1987: 22.
Gross, John. Review of *Weep No More, My Lady*. *New York Times*, 3 July 1987. Sec.
    3, 27.
*Kirkus Reviews*, 15 April 1987: 575.
*Library Journal*, July 1987: 101.
Olson, Kiki. Review of *Weep No More, My Lady*. *New York Times Book Review*, 28
    June 1987: 24.
*Publishers Weekly*, 22 April 1988: 80.
Steinberg, Sybil. Review of *Weep No More, My Lady*. *Publishers Weekly*, 8 May
    1987: 64.
*Wilson Library Bulletin*, September 1987: 23.

## While My Pretty One Sleeps

*Belles Lettres*, 4 (Summer 1989): 33.

Bernikow, Louise. Review of *While My Pretty One Sleeps*. *Cosmopolitan*, May 1989: 50.

*Booklist*, 1 April 1989: 1329.

*Books*, September 1989: 6.

*Books*, September 1989: 15.

Curtin, Jack. Review of *While My Pretty One Sleeps*. *New York Times Book Review*, 18 June 1989: 20.

*Inside Books*, June 1989: 53.

*Kirkus Reviews*, 15 March 1989: 398.

*Los Angeles Times Book Review*, 14 May 1989: 11.

*Los Angeles Times Book Review*, 8 July 1990: 10.

Steinberg, Sybil. Review of *While My Pretty One Sleeps*. *Publishers Weekly*, 31 March 1989: 46.

Toepfer, Susan. "Picks and Pans." *People Weekly*, 26 June 1989: 27.

## The Anastasia Syndrome

*Booklist*, 1 November 1989: 524.

Kent, Bill. Review of *The Anastasia Syndrome*. *New York Times Book Review*, 3 December 1989: 20.

*Kirkus Reviews*, 15 September 1989: 1348.

*Los Angeles Times Book Review*, 3 March 1991: 10.

Mitgang, Herbert. "An Escape from the Present." *New York Times*, 6 December 1989. Sec. 3, 25.

*Publishers Weekly*, 8 February 1991: 55.

Steinberg, Sybil. Review of *The Anastasia Syndrome*. *Publishers Weekly*, 29 September 1989: 61.

Toepfer, Susan. "Picks and Pans." *People Weekly*, 29 January 1990: 28.

## Loves Music, Loves to Dance

Abeel, Erica. "Beach Reads." *New Woman*, July 1991: 32.

Bernikow, Louise. Review of *Loves Music, Loves to Dance*. *Cosmopolitan*, May 1991: 25.

Cohen, Joyce. Review of *Loves Music, Loves to Dance*. *New York Times Book Review*, 16 June 1991: 16.

*Kirkus Reviews*, 15 March 1991: 342.

*Los Angeles Times Book Review*, 9 June 1991: 13.

Schwartz, Gil. "Page-Turning Fool." *Fortune*, 26 August 1991: 113–114.

Steinberg, Sybil. Review of *Loves Music, Loves to Dance. Publishers Weekly*, 5 April
      1991: 138.
Toepfer, Susan. "Picks and Pans." *People Weekly*, 27 May 1991: 25.
*Washington Post Book World*, 12 May 1991: 10.
*Washington Post Book World*, 26 May 1991: 12.


### All Around the Town

*Booklist*, 15 April 1992: 1483.
*Books*, September 1992: 17+.
Donavin, Denise Perry. Review of *All Around the Town. Booklist*, 15 April 1992:
      1483.
*Kirkus Reviews*, 1 April 1992: 410.
Lehmann-Haupt, Christopher. "Two Contrasting Murder Mysteries." *New York
      Times*, 4 June 1992: C18.
*Los Angeles Times Book Review*, 10 May 1992: 8.
Stasio, Marilyn. Review of *All Around the Town. New York Times Book Review*, 10
      May 1992: 23.
Steinberg, Sybil. Review of *All Around the Town. Publishers Weekly*, 30 March 1992:
      91.
Toepfer, Susan. "Picks and Pans." *People Weekly*, 15 June 1992: 28.
*Wall Street Journal*, 1 June 1992: A10.
*Washington Post Book World*, 7 June 1992: 8.


### I'll Be Seeing You

Bard, Nancy. Review of *I'll Be Seeing You. School Library Journal*, November 1993:
      148.
Chase, Chris. "New and Hot in Paperback." *Cosmopolitan*, May 1994: 18.
Seaman, Donna. Review of *I'll Be Seeing You. Booklist*, 15 April 1993: 1469.
Stasio, Marilyn. Review of *I'll Be Seeing You. New York Times Book Review*, 2 May
      1993: 22.
Steinberg, Sybil. Review of *I'll Be Seeing You. Publishers Weekly*, 5 April 1993: 63–
      64.
Toepfer, Susan. "Picks and Pans." *People Weekly*, 31 May 1993: 22–25.


### Remember Me

Steinberg, Sybil. Review of *Remember Me. Publishers Weekly*, 11 April 1994: 54.
Toepfer, Susan. "Picks and Pans." *People Weekly*, 9 May 1994: 35.

## *The Lottery Winner*

Melton, Emily. Review of *The Lottery Winner*. *Booklist*, 15 October 1994: 370.
Steinberg, Sybil. Review of *The Lottery Winner*. *Publishers Weekly*, 17 October 1994: 62.

## *Let Me Call You Sweetheart*

Stasio, Marilyn. Review of *Let Me Call You Sweetheart*. *The New York Times Book Review*, 4 June 1995: 24.

## OTHER SECONDARY SOURCES

Aiken, Joan. "Plot and Character in Suspense Fiction." In *The Writer's Handbook*. Ed. Sylvia K. Burack. Boston: The Writer, 1991: 245–251.
Berger, Arthur Asa. *Cultural Criticism: A Primer of Key Concepts*. Foundations of Popular Culture, Vol. 4. Thousand Oaks, Calif.: Sage Publications, 1995.
Boose, Lynda E. "The Father's House and the Daughter in It: The Structures of Western Culture's Daughter-Father Relationship." In *Daughters and Fathers*. Ed. Lynda E. Boose and Betty S. Flowers. Baltimore: Johns Hopkins University Press, 1989: 19–74.
Cawelti, John G. *Adventure, Mystery, and Romance: Formula Stories as Art and Popular Culture*. Chicago: University of Chicago Press, 1976.
Klein, Kathleen Gregory. "Introduction." In *Great Women Mystery Writers: Classic to Contemporary*. Ed. Kathleen Gregory Klein. Westport, Conn.: Greenwood Press, 1994: 1–9.
Norville, Barbara. *Writing the Modern Mystery*. Cincinnati: Writer's Digest Books, 1986.
Showalter, Elaine. "The Feminist Critical Revolution." In *The New Feminist Criticism: Essays on Women, Literature, and Theory*. Ed. Elaine Showalter. London: Virago Press, 1986: 3–17.
———. "Toward a Feminist Poetics." In *The New Feminist Criticism: Essays on Women, Literature, and Theory*. Ed. Elaine Showalter. London: Virago Press, 1986: 125–143.
Squire, Charles. *Celtic Myths and Legend*. Reprint. *The Mythology of the British Islands*. 1905. Hollywood, Calif.: Newcastle Publishing, 1975.

# Index

**About the Author**

LINDA C. PELZER is Associate Professor of English at Wesley College in Dover, Delaware. A specialist in American literature, she is a former Fulbright scholar. She is currently at work on a study of the work of Gail Godwin.